THE TRUCK STOP

Richard Seveska

THE TRUCK STOP

A Chaplain's Stories

CLAY BRIDGES
PRESS

The Truck Stop
Copyright © 2022 by Richard Seveska. All rights reserved.

Published by Clay Bridges Press in Houston, TX
www.ClayBridgesPress.com
All rights reserved. No part of this publication may be reproduced, stored in a retrieval system, or transmitted in any form by any means, electronic, mechanical, photocopy, recording, or otherwise, without the prior permission of the publisher, except as provided for by USA copyright law.
eISBN: 978-1-68488-013-3 (eBook)
ISBN: 978-1-68488-014-0 (paperback)

DEDICATION

I dedicate this book to Kathy, my wife who died of cancer after forty-six years of marriage. She had inspired me to write the stories based on my years of experience at the truck stop.

I also dedicate this work to the truck drivers without whom there would be no stories or food on our tables. And to the employees of the truck stops that recognize the need in their customers and try to take care of them by guiding the chaplain to the people with most need.

This dedication would not be complete without the love and support of JoAnn, my wife of three years. She has been my inspiration to complete the story convincing me to publish this inspiring book.

Thanks, Jo, for your love and inspiration.

TABLE OF CONTENTS

PREFACE

Michael O'Toole is an ordained Catholic Deacon and a Truck Stop Chaplain. Mike, as he prefers to be called, was ordained at Holy Name Cathedral in Chicago, Illinois in 1987, and has been serving his church community in a suburb of Chicago for twenty-two years.

A few years ago, the US Conference of Catholic Bishops realized that there were over eight million truck drivers on the road every day. So, the Bishops challenged deacons and others to serve the people of God who traveled the highways and byways of this nation. Once Michael heard about the need for ministers at the truck stop, he immediately felt compelled to help with this ministry.

He discovered that truck drivers are continuously on the move, and they are often on the road on Sunday morning to make their first delivery early Monday morning. He also realized they needed help.

Mike is sixty-six years old and has now been a truck stop chaplain for twelve years. He had decided years ago that for him to really be Christian meant that he had to be with those who really needed help. His wife Mandy and he had been involved in several ministries, including Baptism Preparation, Marriage Preparation, and others, which prepared them to work with people on a one on one basis. He was ready for another ministry but couldn't find one that worked for him.

He needed to feel like he belonged and needed to be happy with what he did. When he had been approached about serving the truck stop ministry, he instantly said yes, because he sensed that this was the one for him.

Over the years, he kept notes of the events and the type of stories from the truck stop. Years later, after reviewing those notes, he decided to write a book of stories based on his experience.

1

THE SHOT

Tim recalled when he had started driving a truck and remembered the enthusiasm he felt. It was a new experience, one that promised to give him a lot of freedom.

As they sat together in a booth at the truck stop, he said to the chaplain, "I thought there would be no boss looking over my shoulder. I would be able to run at my own pace and check-in to let *them* know where I was."

To Tim it sounded like a great life. Less frustration, no pressure, no deadlines—just drive the truck and get paid for sitting on his backside. That quickly evaporated as he learned there are definite deadlines and delivery times. The pressure was quite intense from customers and from dispatchers. And as for the boss; he now had GPS tracking and digital printouts in the truck to help manage the loads and keep an eye on the driver's schedules. Tim thought to himself, *It's just like the line in the movie, "1984," Big Brother is watching.*

Tim now lived in a quiet little community near Indianapolis, Indiana, with Sheryl, his wife of twenty-two years and their three children. They lived in a comfortable home with four bedrooms and plenty of room for their family. At the time of the incident, he had been only thirty years old and in pretty good shape for a trucker. He had kept an exercise mat in the truck that he pulled out to do sit-ups on a regular basis.

That was how Tim started telling his story to Michael, the Truck Stop Chaplain who looked very welcoming and was dressed rather casually in Khaki slacks and a plain white chaplain shirt with the Truck Stop Chaplain title embroidered over the left breast pocket. He also wore a gray cardigan sweater that kind of matched his thinning salt and pepper gray hair (To be honest, he was almost bald on top of his head).

Mike noticed that Tim's light colored hair and muscular build made him look like Jeff Bridges, the actor. Tim was neatly dressed in a clean pair of jeans and a short-sleeved shirt. Even now, in his forties, Tim didn't look overweight like some truckers did.

He told Mike, "It's tough to keep from gaining weight when you sit around in the truck all day on your backside."

Tim had been driving a truck for eighteen years and loved the relative freedom and the income that driving provided, but traveling alone was really hard on him and his family. He usually had to leave on Sunday morning to get to his first drop or pick-up on Monday. That meant he usually didn't get to attend church on

Sunday with his family. In reality he felt this was okay, because he wasn't very religious anyway.

He traveled all over the country during the week and tried to get home on weekends, but only managed to reach that goal about fifty percent of the time. Sometimes, he was out on the road for two or three weeks, and when he got home, it was usually on Friday. Often, it was on Saturday, and he would have to leave again on Sunday. This didn't make for a happy home life, even when he told his wife, "I only get paid when the truck is moving."

She had begun to hate that phrase, but realized it was true. They really needed his job more than ever, to pay the bills they had racked up due to the rough pregnancy with their son, who was only three months old. And of course, some of those doctor bills were not covered under their insurance.

When on the road, Tim really missed his family, the healthy meals his wife provided, and the comfort of being at home and the warmth of his own bed. Most of all he missed the hugs and kisses from his daughters (and his wife) and being able to play with his son. Being on the road all the time could be a terribly lonely existence.

There were also many times when things came up, and Sheryl would call him on his cell phone to tell him something about the kids or that something or other in the house had broken. But he wasn't able to be there to help, and those were the times that hurt the most. He had found it very difficult to keep the relationship with his spouse going when he couldn't be there. He had heard the statistic that truck drivers have one of the highest divorce rates of any profession. So, he used his cell phone to call her frequently. He figured an ounce of prevention was worth…(Well you know).

Then Tim leaned in toward the chaplain and lowered his voice. This indicated that it was a very personal story and probably not often shared. Mike noticed that Tim's face took on a very serious look as he continued.

"About fifteen years ago, I was traveling along one of the interstate routes, hauling a twenty-ton load of vegetables in a reefer [a refrigerated truck]. This was one of those trips when I had *not* gotten home on the weekend, even for a couple of hours. I was dog-tired and hungry after an eleven-hour day in traffic, and the road had turned into a blur of dark lanes with white lines and dashes that had a hypnotizing effect on me, at seventy miles per hour. I realized that I'd better stop for something to eat and get some rest, or I would end up in a ditch or worse."

He told Mike, that it had been an early fall night, and he had seen an unbelievable sunset and an incredible orange full moon rise then duck behind a dark cloud cover. The air was quite cool at 40 degrees and there was light fog in low areas, but it was otherwise very clear.

"The fog and the cool heavy air made everything damp and full of dew. I was thinking to myself, *The hypnotizing effect of the road and the lack of sleep are making me…*" Tim said.

"All of a sudden, I was quickly snapped back to reality when a car passed me at a much higher rate of speed. I looked down and discovered I had slowed to only fifty miles per hour and was drifting off to the side of the road, where warning bumps were causing a rumbling sound in my truck. I had to get off the road now!"

There was almost no traffic at 1:00 am on that Monday morning as he pulled off the highway ramp to a truck stop. He had put himself on a weird schedule to avoid most of the traffic from the cities, which meant that he was eating and sleeping at strange hours. This time the plan had not worked because an accident had stopped traffic for a couple of hours. The last few hours had finally been clear sailing and allowed him to log some miles. It was times like that where he was painfully aware that he only got paid by the mile. So, all that time he had just spent in a traffic jam was basically for no pay. He said to himself, *And why am I doing this?* Of course, he knew, this was the only job where he could make a living with his limited training.

The truck stop was not one of the huge ones, but had the necessary items like restrooms, food, and fuel. Tim thought, *Oh, what I wouldn't do for a cup of coffee!* Luck was not with him on that night; the lot was full, so he started to pull out and back onto the interstate on-ramp. He paused at the stop sign for a few moments thinking, *What should I do?* and realized that not only had he reached his legal limit of hours for the day, but he was also incredibly beat, really hungry, and near his own physical limits. He had not eaten all day and would need to stop very soon to satisfy that gnawing hunger, or he would end up with one of those raging headaches that made it feel like his eyes were about to pop out.

He often got them when he didn't eat correctly. So, he decided to go to the on-ramp and pull over there to rest.

In some states parking on the shoulder of the ramps is illegal and can get you a ticket and a huge fine. Luckily, it was allowed in this state. It sometimes became a decision between which fine you wanted; one for parking or one for being over the limit of hours. And there was always the risk of having an accident when you tried to drive when you were overly tired.

He thought about his wife and two daughters at home all warm and snuggled in their beds, and that thought made him all the more tired. He had called home at about 9:00 p.m. and talked to Sheryl and both young daughters. He liked to call home when he was away, because it was the only way to stay in touch. His daughters and his new son were also such a joy to him.

Tim continued his story by telling Mike, "I would rather have been at home with my family that night, but I need to make a living.

"So there I was, '*On the road again.*' which I often sing to myself. Just like Johnny Cash." As he turned his eighteen-wheeler toward the onramp and pulled over to the side, he noticed a four-wheeler (a trucker term for a car), was pulled over in front of him. A very attractive young lady of about twenty-five years old, with long blond hair and a short skirt, had the hood up and was looking at the engine of a white car. The car was at least fifteen years old and had peeling paint spots all over, exposing the grey primer.

Tim slipped on his winter coat and got out of his truck with the spare set of keys in his right hand. He automatically locked the doors, because his wallet was in the truck and the engine was still running. He also left the headlights on, so that he could see the car in front of him.

He called to the woman and asked if she needed some help. She looked nervous, and she nodded her head, as she shouted back, "My car just stopped and won't start."

He asked, "Can I take a look at it?" and she said, "Yes. Please help me."

As he started to walk the ten feet toward her, he remembered that he had a flashlight in the truck. He turned and started to go back to get it. As he approached the front of the truck, he saw something out of the corner of his eye and turned to see what it was. It was the woman's male accomplice coming up out of the weeds on the other side of the ramp with something long in his hands, and he realized this was a set-up.

Tim said, "God, please help me."

The man in the grass shouted something, then Tim heard the blast and felt the searing white-hot pain in his side.

He thought, *This is it. I'm dead.*

The shotgun blast spun him around, even though it had not made a direct hit; it caught him between the left arm and the waist. He was immediately thrown against the front fender of the truck by a force that felt like he had been hit by a raging bull. He went crashing to the ground, but was somehow saved and miraculously still alive, even though he knew he was losing a lot of blood. Somehow, he was not in a lot of pain, which scared him even more. He thought, *Isn't this how it is just before people die, they have no more pain?*

He heard the woman scream, "You didn't have to shoot him!"

"He was going to get away," the gunman said.

Tim prepared himself to meet his maker. He was certain the gunman would shoot him again to prevent an eye-witness from identifying him. He lay very still, held his breath, and forced his eyes open without blinking, so that he would not attract attention.

The gunman looked at him and said, "I think he's dead."

He checked Tim's back pockets and discovered there was no wallet. Then he checked the front pockets for keys. Finding none, he said, "We'd better get out of here."

Mike was now able to see his assailant but couldn't see many details. The man had dark clothing and a stocking cap on his head. He and the woman both quickly got in the car and sped off, but Tim was able to get the license plate number.

He lay there for a moment then tried to get up; there was some pain, but nothing intense. He knew that at 1:00 a.m. on a Monday morning, there was not likely to be much traffic on this section of road, and he was far enough from the truck stop and the highway that no one would have seen what was happening. With all of the noise of the idling truck engines at the truck stop, it was not likely that any other drivers would have heard the noise or have thought anything of it. They would think, *Probably just a backfire.*

Tim knew he had to get up and get to the truck stop to get help or he would surely die right there.

At first he crawled, and then somehow, as he prayed for help, he was able to find the strength to stand and limp up the ramp. He got only a few steps, when a state trooper came rushing to his aid. Apparently, another trucker was awake in his truck, had heard the shotgun blast, and called the police on his CB radio.

The State Trooper had been only a mile down the road at the time and showed up at the same time as the trucker who made the call. An ambulance came within only a couple of minutes and took Tim to a local hospital, which was surprisingly close by. He had been able to give the State Trooper the license plate number before passing out.

On the way to the hospital, he was again conscious, but heard the EMT telling the dispatcher, "This one is a really bad shotgun wound. Better prepare for the worst situation."

Tim passed out thinking, *That's it! I am dying.*

Luck was with him, because the hospital was big enough to be able to deal with his gunshot wound. The shotgun pattern was only about four inches around, because he was so close to the shooter. In addition, Tim's cell phone was in the pocket of his winter coat, which helped to deflect a portion of the blast between his arm and his waist.

The doctor later told Tim, "Had that shot been a couple of inches further to the right, it would have been all over."

The couple was apprehended and later convicted of attempted murder, armed robbery, and other charges.

Tim's incident on the highway had happened fifteen years ago, and he was all healed now, but he told the story with moist eyes. He was thankful that he had been spared that night, and because of it, he had found a renewed faith in God.

He said, "That night on the interstate, when I saw the gunman out of the corner of my eye, I had said, 'God, please help me,' just as the gunman fired his shot. God did help me. The doctors were amazed that I was not dead when I arrived at the hospital. They had never seen anyone survive a shotgun blast and live."

Tim later found out that the gunman panicked when Tim turned to go back to his truck for the flashlight. So, the gunman pulled the trigger in his panic, when he thought Tim was going to get away. As he pulled the trigger, he slipped in the dew laden tall grass he was hiding in, which caused him to miss his target.

The couple thought that truckers carried large sums of money to pay for fuel, and they were hoping to take advantage of a driver and rob him at gunpoint. Tim told Mike that he never carried large sums of money; he paid for everything on credit cards.

Tim told the chaplain, "I have not been able to talk about the incident with anyone in detail. Thank you for taking the time to discuss it with me. God Bless you, Mike! Please keep being here for us drivers. We really need this. I now know that the Lord is always there for me, so, I keep a Bible on the seat next to me in the truck."

Mike and Tim talked for at least an hour more about Tim's family, God, and faith. Mike asked him if they could pray. He said, "Yes, please do!" Mike put his hands on top of Tim's across the table as he said a prayer. He gave Tim a blessing and said good-bye. They both left the truck stop that night with their spirits lifted, and were both filled with the Lord's presence in their lives.

Tim told the chaplain, "I have not been able to talk to anyone about this story, but because you have taken the time to care, I was able to share my feelings with you. I can't tell you how much that helps me."

Mike later told his wife Mandy that Tim's story was rather dramatic; it demonstrated the need to be careful on the road, but the Lord works in our lives, if we only recognize Him and ask for His help.

He also told her that this was not a typical truck stop story, as most of them were about what happened on the road between a couple of vehicles or about their family, but he had discovered that their stories were as diverse as there were people to tell them.

2

THE ACCIDENT

On another night Mike met Sam, who looked like an average man (not your stereotypical trucker, whatever that is). He looked like he was tall (at least in his upper body) as he was seated in the booth. He was about fifty years old with thinning, well-trimmed, salt-n-pepper hair. He also had a thin, clean-shaven, corporate-looking face with kind eyes and an inviting smile.

Mike noticed that Sam was also dressed a little too sharply for a typical truck driver in what looked like a pair of dress pants and a dress shirt. He thought to himself, *How often do you see that?*

Sam started cautiously answering the usual questions. "Where are you from? What's your name?" etc… Mike didn't think Sam was a driver, so he asked him, "Are you a driver?"

Sam told him that he had just come from a company dinner. That's why he was dressed so fancy.

Sam then lowered his voice and said,

"Do you have some time? I need to tell you something."

"I sure do," said Mike.

"Please have a seat."

Mike slid into the other side of the booth, put his book down, and looked attentively at the man.

He continued with the fact that he had been thirty-two years old at the time the incident happened. He was driving down a four–lane highway at ten o'clock on a Friday evening. He was not in a big hurry, but was heading home after two long weeks on the road.

Sam certainly preferred to be home on the weekends with Sarah, his wife of eight years. He also had two children; redheaded and freckled, Rachel who was seven and his four-year-old son, Brad, who was a ball of action with his flyaway blond hair and endless supply of energy. Sam loved his wife and children and missed them terribly on these trips that lasted so long.

Sam had been an owner-operator until a year ago when the cost of everything went sky high and he had to get rid of his rig and become a company driver. Sam now drove a company truck and, even though he was getting less pay per mile, he actually made more take-home-pay because he did not have to pay all of the bills and expenses for the truck. He jokingly said, "It's so nice to be able to just call 1-800-fix-it, whenever I have trouble with the truck, and someone else pays the bill."

Both men laughed, and then Sam continued with his story.

On the night this happened, it was a clear, warm summer evening just before midnight, not humid, but the kind of idyllic warm night, around seventy degrees, that was etched in all of our memories as a perfect night.

"It would have been a great night to be at home in my own bed, enjoying the summer night breeze," Sam said with a pleasant smile.

He was now on the backside of the trip, heading toward home and was only one hundred miles away. The truck had been running well with no troubles. He was thinking that it would be great to get back home, when a deer jumped in front of his truck, out of nowhere. It was a huge six-point buck with a bright bushy white tail, which Sam remembered glowed in the headlights. He hit the brakes and tried to safely swerve to avoid an accident. It was too late. The deer hit the truck in the front right corner, which caused his truck to blow a tire and roll over on its right side. Sam could see it all happening in slow motion, and he knew he was in deep trouble as he said to himself, "This is really going to hurt."

Sam was not a religious person, nor was he used to praying. He went with his wife and family to church once in a great while and more often used the excuse that he needed to be on the road on Sunday, so he couldn't go to church. He admitted to the chaplain that he was just being lazy, and the truth was that he never felt the need for God in his life, so he felt no need to go to church.

"That was for them church folk," he told Mike.

On that particular Friday evening, as his semi-tractor-trailer truck slid across the highway on its right side, Sam cried out loud, "Lord, please help me!"

Just then, his truck hit the guardrail of an overpass and the cab portion of the truck slipped over the edge. Hanging there, injured, bleeding, and half-conscious, Sam thought he would soon die. He would bleed to death, the truck would fall with him in it, or it would burst into flames at any moment. He tried to move but felt a piece of metal jabbing into his leg, preventing its removal.

All of a sudden, Sam could hear someone talking to him from outside the broken driver side window. Sam turned his head, opened his eyes, and concentrated on listening.

A young man at the window opening with kind, soothing eyes, said,

"Just relax, my name is Josh, and I'm here to help you. I'll go around and come in the passenger side."

Mike was surprised that he was able to see the man's soft blue eyes at all in the dark.

Before he knew it, Josh was on the other side and said, "Just relax and let me take care of you."

"Thank you, but don't we have to get out of here?"

"It's all under control. We got a call for help."

Sam thought that was a strange thing to say, but the young man applied a pressure bandage to his neck wound to stop the bleeding. He held Sam's hand to comfort him and stayed with him. He told Sam that the rest of the crew would be there soon to free him from the wreckage. Sure enough, Sam soon heard the wail of a siren, and the young man said, "I have to go outside now, but I won't be far from you."

In a couple of minutes, another man appeared at the window. After getting some information from Sam, he quickly cut the metal away to get Sam out of the wreckage. Then he helped Sam out onto a ladder attached to a fire truck that quickly moved them away from the wreckage. Within a minute or two after they were clear, the wreckage of the truck fell twenty feet to the pavement below and completely smashed the cab Sam had been in.

The big, burley EMT that had helped him from the wreckage asked Sam, "Who bandaged your head and neck wounds?"

"It was one of your boys named Josh. He was in the cab with me when the rest of you came roaring up with your sirens blaring."

"Sir, we don't have anyone named Josh, and we don't have any advanced team. Another trucker called us, and we got here when you heard the sirens."

"But, Josh said he would be right outside."

"There were no other medical personnel here when we got here. There was no ladder in place and no one could have climbed over that wreckage to get to you."

"That's impossible. He was with me in the cab."

"Sir, that's not possible as there was no room in the cab for anyone but you. The crash had pushed the other side of the passenger compartment against you."

It was then that Sam remembered that he had prayed, "Lord, please help me."

Sam knew right then that the Lord really did help him, and it has since changed his life. He now tried to get to church every Sunday, and if he really couldn't go because of work, he would pray as he drove.

Sam said to the chaplain with reddened eyes, "I feel much happier and at peace now that I have felt the healing presence of the Lord. I know He really is always there and ready to help if we only ask."

Sam was shaking and had tears in his eyes. After he paused for a moment to get control of his emotions, he said, "God bless you, Mike. You have to keep being here for us truckers. I have told that story to a very few people, because most would say that I was making it up. Or, nothing like that ever happens. But, with you, Mike, I have been able to tell the whole story including how it has changed me."

Mike talked with Sam some more and said, "It appears that the Lord has something else in mind for you."

"What do you mean?"

"Do you agree that the Lord spared your life?"

"I definitely do!"

"Well, maybe you should be telling your story to more of the people you meet. And if they are willing to listen, tell them all of it, as a witness to God's love for us. You just might change some hearts along the way."

"You know, you're right. I'll do that. It's the least I can do."

As he left the truck stop, Mike looked up and said, "This was a really good night. Lord, thank you for your Spirit!"

3

WHAT IS A TRUCK STOP?

M ike often reviewed what happened at the truck stop each night with Mandy, his soul-mate. She was the mother of their two children and still looked like the bride he married almost forty years ago. At least that's what he thought. She did not actively participate in his ministry, but she was interested and attentive in these reviews. Mike found it very helpful to go over the important details of the most interesting meetings for each night at the truck stop.

She would typically ask, "How was trucking?" and Mike would unfold his stories from the night.

One night she asked, "What is a truck stop?"

He explained that a truck stop was a place for truck drivers to get fuel (usually diesel) much like a gas station. But, it was also where they could get food for their bodies and other services meant specifically for them.

These other services usually included a game room, a large screen TV room, and hot showers. Most truck stops also have a store where they can purchase items for their truck, for their personal needs, for the road, or even office supplies.

Other truck stops offer even more for the driver's convenience and enjoyment. Things like a barbershop, a truck repair shop, a Laundromat, and several restaurants in the same building. The restaurants often include a sit-down section with waitresses and one or more fast food establishments. These things are especially important, since the drivers practically live in their trucks. So, this oasis is a home-away-from-home for these lonely souls.

There is even one that claims to be "The Largest Truck Stop in The World," located on I-80 in eastern Iowa. This particular truck stop has spaces to park 800 trucks. It has a huge sit-down restaurant and a food court, like the one you might find at a large shopping mall. The store section is so large that there is a full size 18-wheeler tractor-trailer (semi) inside, along one end of the store with two full sized semi tractors at the other end.

Besides truck parts and trucker office supplies, truck stops also have some very unique items in their stores. One of those items is named a Heater Meal, which conjures up thoughts of a contraption you might hang on your vehicle's engine to get enough heat to cook the meal.

He told his wife that he had once purchased one of those meals to see just what it was. When he investigated the packaging and read the directions inside, he found that you only needed to add water to the aluminum pan and a chemical reaction causes heat to be internally generated, which warms the meal. He said to Mandy, "Ah, the wonders of modern technology!"

Another item of amazement to Mike was the insulated drinking mug. This probably doesn't sound amazing as we have all seen them or have purchased one of them for our own use before. "Yeah, you have twenty-seven of them." Mandy quipped. Most of which Mike had been given by companies with their logo emblazoned on them, because he also had his own business. Companies must think we would certainly purchase their product after seeing it advertised on an insulated mug, wouldn't you? These companies select a mug to advertise their product with the idea that to have one of these mugs must fulfill one of humankind's greatest needs, or so it would seem.

However, the insulated drinking mugs at a truck stop are so large that you think there must be a group of giants that frequent this place and you start wondering if there is there a beanstalk nearby. Some of these mugs can hold up to a gallon of liquid or more. Actually for a trucker, this can be very practical, because once they get on the road, they don't want to stop. They want to keep earning money in the hours they have.

Akin to other settings, there was a video rental section of the truck stop store, containing movies for your entertainment. There was a "Books on Tape" section. As with video rentals, truckers could rent a CD-ROM containing a voice track with someone reading a book to them as they drive along the highway, and when they were done with the book, they could drop it off at the next truck stop.

4

THE HILLS

The first time Mike went to the truck stop on his own, as a Chaplain, he took a route that was kind of twisty and hilly. You know the kind, where the yellow triangular signs have a snake like figure printed on them as a warning. While snakes were not his worst fear, they definitely got his attention. So, you might say for him it was a double warning to the dangers ahead (snakes or curvy roads).

It was daylight on a warm fall afternoon. The sunshine made the brightly colored leaves of the season glow in the sunny rays. As he drove, there were a few driveways sparsely dotted along that stretch of winding suburban road. The hilly nature of the road did not let his mind wander and demanded attention. The radio was turned down low (his wife would be first to say, "That was a phenomenon in of itself, for him to turn *down* the radio") and he was thinking about his introduction into the truck stop ministry. In his thoughts he asked the Lord, *Do you think I will be any good at this new ministry to truckers? After all what do I know about these people or their work?*

Just then, his car came over a small hill in the road, and he noticed an older four-door car in the opposite lane with a young couple. The driver had tried to make a turn into a driveway at the bottom of the hill on the other side of the road. He had overshot the driveway and ended up with the front end of his car in the ditch next to the drive and the back end of the car hanging into the roadway. Mike observed this all happening as he traveled at forty-five miles per hour. Then, out of the corner of his eye, he suddenly saw someone sitting in the passenger seat of his own car. He quickly turned to look and saw that it was his brother who had died in an accident with a truck almost twenty-five years ago. His brother was three years older, but he and Dennis had been very close, and the loss of his brother was absolutely devastating.

The sight of his brother frightened him, and in his surprise, he pulled the steering wheel toward the right and instinctively hit the brakes at the same time. These actions pulled his car off the road, which he felt in the steering. His attention was ripped back to the road and the crash that he surely would be facing.

Instead, he saw a huge eighteen-wheeler (semi-truck) was now bearing down on that car, from over the hill. The truck driver was trying to avoid hitting the car in the ditch, and his tires were pluming a cloud of blue smoke as he tried to stop, but because Mike's car was stopped and off the road, the truck driver was able to miss the car in the ditch by using Mike's lane.

The truck passed safely between the two cars. The other car quickly backed out and departed, and Mike turned to his brother, who was no longer there. Mike was shaking and emotionally rattled. So, after a few minutes, he said out loud with a shaky voice, "Okay, Lord, I guess you really do want me at the truck stop." He was still shaking when he put his car in drive and continued on his way.

While driving, Mike thought, *I know this is a could-a-been, but there would surely have been a huge accident with that truck and both of our cars. So, I guess you answered me Lord and let me know in a definite way that I am needed at the truck stop. It also seems that you will tell me what I need to know. I leave it in your hands.*

As Mike drove up to the truck stop, he saw the truck parking lot with spaces for over one hundred of the behemoth sixty-five-foot eighteen-wheeled monsters that would soon be resting there for the night. Some of the spaces were already filled, and several trucks turned off the highway with him.

When he got out of his car at the truck stop, Mike paused for a moment, and one of the first things he noticed was the sounds and the scents of the place. He heard a continuous deep rumbling from the trucks as a backdrop, the sound of crying tires from the nearby highway and the smell of diesel fuel. Then, as he walked through the doors, he sensed the smell of strong coffee and fried onions. When the automatic door closed behind him with a swish, the rumbling of idling diesel truck engines was muted and replaced with a more subdued clinking of knives, forks, and the rattle of plates, cups, and saucers as they were placed on the counter and table tops.

Conversation was muted, too. Men and women had traveled countless miles before arriving at this place, and their faces showed the fatigue from concentrating on the ribbons of highway they had traveled.

Mike would later discover that truck stop ministry was very fulfilling, because the truckers responded with such positive and welcoming acceptance to him and this ministry of presence. After all, these were people who spent the majority of their lives alone. Mike found that the truckers were 'blown away' that a minister had taken the time to listen to them and to prompt them to tell him their stories.

5

ON THE MOVE

Like all of us, truck drivers suffer from loneliness, family crises, and pain that can sear the soul. Truckers have a more difficult family life because they are on the road most of the time. And like us, they become frightened and overwhelmed, so they will reach out for help if only someone will offer it without judging. Sometimes, however, help needs to be offered more than once, and other times, it needs to be offered many times. Mike found this true with John.

John was sitting by himself at the corner of the restaurant counter, looking engrossed in his menu. Walking by, as usual, Mike said hello. There was no response except a nod of sorts, and the man quickly looked down. Mike had learned that, despite the worry in the man's face, the body language had just said, *I don't want to talk.*

But Mike wasn't one to give up easily, and he came back a little later and got the same message. The third time, he decided not to say anything to the man and was surprised when John said, "Sit down, chaplain. I want to talk to you."

As Mike sat down, he noticed the worry he had seen earlier was etched deeply into the rugged face before him. The man was about thirty-five or forty years old. He had not shaven for at least 24 to 48 hours and had dark uncombed hair. The dark unshaven look and the man's stocky body completed the visual picture for the chaplain, as someone under great strain.

Mike had learned that this was a more typical truck driver. He also learned that truck drivers tended to be similar to the factory workers he had met through his business connections. Most of them were hard working individuals who wore 'work clothes,' which consisted of jeans and a heavy shirt meant to last through the toughest work assignments. Some of them had company shirts with their names sewn on the breast pockets.

The man's eyes said it all and the rest of his face said, "I am depressed, please help me." He was looking at Mike through his deep sad eyes, as he said quietly, "Cora, my wife of six months, has disappeared. I called the house, but there was no answer. I've called a neighbor, and they said that my wife has gone and taken the new car and some furniture. I'm really worried. What can I do? I'm very tired, but I feel I need to get back in the truck and drive straight through for eight more hours to get home."

Mike realized the dire nature of the man's problem. He had just finished an eleven-hour run, and he looked as tired and stressed as he could be.

Mike thought to himself, *If he gets in his truck feeling like he does and attempts to drive for another eight hours, there's a high probability that he would get into a serious accident. I can't imagine reading the newspaper tomorrow to find that he had crashed into a bus full of kids, or some equally horrible fate.*

How could Mike advise him? What could he possibly say to help him? Then, an idea came to him. Mike instantly thought, *I'm sure this is from the Holy Spirit.*

Mike asked John, "Are you a church-going man?

He looked at Mike with a funny expression and replied, "I have been to church a couple of times."

Mike asked, "Do you know your pastor well enough to call him?"

Looking perplexed, John said, "No. Are you kidding? Why would I do that?"

Mike told him, "You're here and he's there. Perhaps the pastor might be able to find your wife and help with the immediate problem as well as start some resolution on the bigger problem of why she left."

John thought about it for a moment and decided to give it a try.

While they waited, John told Mike his name and where he was from, as well as how long he had been a driver.

Twenty minutes and some cell-phone calls later, the pastor John had contacted was able to reach John's wife and was already starting the healing process.

"I found your wife. She doesn't want to talk to you, but I think we can work on it when you get back," the pastor told John on the phone.

As both men walked out to John's truck, he had hope in his voice and not so much dread.

He said, "I think I will rest here for the night and start for home in the morning."

"Thank you for being here for me. You have helped me pull my life together. God Bless you!" John said with a smile.

Mike thought, *This ministry of presence is not magic! It is people helping other people with daily problems. Some of that help comes from listening to people as they figure out their own solutions.*

Mike also knew that he could not do this without help from the Holy Spirit.

6

TRUCKER'S NEEDS

O ver the years as a chaplain in the truck stop, Mike had heard many stories like John's. One of the things that helped was the acceptance by the truckers and the truck stop staff. The staff personnel could see the results on the truckers' faces and often pointed out people that might need help. The results of those encounters have encouraged the staff members to also seek out the chaplain for support in their own needs.

Mike offered Bibles to the drivers, which amazingly went very quickly, demonstrating that these people were hungry for comfort and for the word of God. They were hungry for inspiration and the knowledge that they had not been forgotten regardless of how alone they may have felt.

Michael had learned that you need to be able to do three things—listen, listen, and listen. In order to listen, however, you have to get to the point where someone is willing to talk, so you cannot be timid in approaching people. You have to be able to walk up to their table and say, "Hi! I'm the chaplain here, and I'm just stopping by to say hello. My name is Mike. What's yours?"

Once you know their name, you can use it to address questions to them, and it helps you remember their name. This is the first step in making a real difference in a person's life. It gets them talking about themselves.

Most people in this ministry to truckers also have to work for a living, and the ministry skills learned at the truck stop are directly transferable to their everyday lives in communicating with their spouse, their family, the people at work, and everyone they come in contact with.

Mike said to his wife, "If I can find a way to talk with the people at the truck stop, then I will have less trouble talking with everyone. I just need to learn to listen and ask the right questions."

The people chaplains encounter do not require a lot from them, except their willingness to be present, to listen, and be willing to talk about their faith (not to shove it down their throats). Sometimes, they look for the chaplain to suggest that God is working in their life in the midst of their stories. They look to Chaplains to help them find the meaning that God may have placed in their lives.

In Mike's personal life, he found that family, co-workers, and customers all responded positively when he actively listened and asked questions about their needs. The response was much less when he partly listened then spouted off about something he was thinking about.

Mike felt God was working in a very real way through him. Although with God's help he may inspire, he was amazed at how inspired and faith-filled he became when helping people. He discovered that diesel fuel, over-brewed coffee, grilled onions, and the clink of cutlery were the scents and sounds of a truly wonderful church.

From the numerous stories Mike had heard at the truck stop, he found family stories, love stories, drama, tragedy, legal battles, crime, intrigue, stories of the road and stories of faith.

Everyone was usually friendly and wanting to talk. Truck drivers were not scary people as some people thought. Many conversations were very politically or financially oriented, but Mike didn't like to engage in that type of discussion and looked for ways to move them into a personal or spiritual realm without controlling the conversations.

There was also irony. Most truckers 'lived' in their truck for instance (They often refer to it as 'The Metal Box'). In order to conserve money, companies install a sleeper attached to the rear of the cab. This allows the driver to sleep in the truck for the required ten hours each day. In order to keep from freezing in the winter or being roasted in the summer, they run the truck engine on idle. This uses a minimum of fuel. However, in some states, it is illegal to run the truck engine on idle while they sleep, unless they have a pet aboard.

Mike said to a driver, "Let's see if I have this in perspective. It's not okay to run the truck engine to keep the human driver from freezing, but it is okay to run the truck to keep a pet comfortable?"

"That's right."

"What is that all about? Doesn't it seem that we have our priorities a little mixed up?"

Mike found out that drivers who travel to those restrictive states get a pet, even if it is only a gold fish.

The driver told Mike, "There are other solutions to the problem of course, but that might make too much sense for the government to attempt. One solution is to install window-fitting tubes that bring heating, air conditioning, television, and other services to each truck. It requires money to install the systems, and that requires a decision to actually solve the problem, not just blame the truckers. I know, we shouldn't start down that path, but come on!"

The chaplain agreed with the driver, and they talked about it for some time.

When Mike got home later that evening, Mandy asked her husband how it went, and Mike told her some of the stories and shared his feelings with her. This was a very important part of the process, which helped him to sort it all out and often lead to new awareness and insights when Mandy made a few suggestions or comments in support of the ministry.

7

THE OLD MAN

Dean was a large man about thirty-five years old with a large frame. He looked the part of truck driver with jeans that looked like they had seen better days and a heavy shirt with signs of wear and a spill or two, but he did have a full head of hair and a clean-shaven face.

Dean sat at the counter and told Mike he was single and lived in Michigan. He wasn't a churchgoer, but truly liked to talk to the Lord as he drove along. Dean told Mike that a couple of months ago he was cruising down a two-lane road on a dark moonless night with the windows open. He had just gotten off the cell-phone with his father, who had offered to front him the money to get a special front-end protector for his truck. It was made of pipe and was designed to protect the truck against collisions with animals. This was especially important because he often traveled on small, two-lane roads at night making deliveries.

After the phone call he was in conversation with the Lord about his day and the tight schedule he was given. Actually, he was complaining to the Lord about all he had to do. These conversations with the Lord were a normal activity for Dean, and it helped him pass the time and get through the next day. He also asked the Lord for protection and guidance in getting the front-end protector. All of a sudden, a deer jumped in front of his truck. He hit the brakes and swerved, but the deer glanced off the right-front corner of the vehicle before Dean could stop. Luckily, he had been able to almost stop before hitting the deer, and he kept the truck under control as he came to a full stop. He knew that he was many miles from any town or service station.

He was in shock for a moment but soon jumped out of the truck to assess the damage. The damage to his truck was not severe, but bad enough to push the bumper into the tire. The tire was not damaged, but the bumper would prevent the tire to rotate freely in a turn. There had not been any other traffic and no one around, nor could he see any lights from any homes that might be nearby. He also tried his cell phone but got the message, *No Service.*

As he surveyed the damage, he started to talk to the Lord out loud, "Lord, what the hell happened here? I thought you were going to protect me like a brother. And now this deer jumped in front of me, damaging my truck and delaying me even further. How am I going to get this fixed at three o'clock in the morning? *Where were you when I needed you?*"

Dean told Mike that he had said many more things to the Lord in anger, which he was not proud of, and would not want to repeat.

Dean was looking at the damage, when out of the darkness, a deep voice said, "How can I help?"

Dean was frightened. Was that the voice of God? What was God going to do with him after all that he had said? Then he saw an older man walking toward him in the headlight beams. The old man looked like a farmer in a pair of bib-front denim coveralls. He had medium-length pure white hair and a short white beard. Dean was frightened at first, but as the old man got closer, he could see the man was very kind and friendly looking.

The man continued, "I saw the whole thing. You didn't have a chance. That buck had your number, and hitting your truck didn't even stop him."

Dean looked around and sure enough, the deer was nowhere to be seen. He was dumbfounded and asked the man, "Where did you come from?"

"I was out for a walk, just beyond your sight. How can I help?"

"Well, I need to get back on the road, but the bumper is bent into the tire."

The old man volunteered that together they might be able to pull the bumper out and free the tire. Well, after a couple of tries, without success, the man said he would call his son and have him bring the pick-up with a chain.

He reached into his coverall pocket and pulled out an older cell phone and made the call. It was no more than five minutes until the son pulled up. In the meantime

Dean and the old man had a great conversation. They talked about Dean's family and the fact that they had just told him they would pay for the front-end protector. The old man told him that he lived on a farm not far from where they stood and understood about unexpected things. He also said that he had raised a huge flock of sheep for a very long time.

The son pulled up with a beat-up, faded red pick-up and the required chain. He was a young man in his thirties and had a slim build with medium-length, uncombed dark brown hair, and he wore jeans and a T-shirt.

They hooked the chain around the corner of the bumper and pulled it out with the son's vehicle. Dean offered them some money, but they refused it, saying that they were glad they could help him.

After they said their good-byes, Dean said, "God Bless you!" to both of them.

And they responded with something he thought was strange. The old man said, "Thank you. You *are* blessed my son!"

As he drove away, Dean looked for any indication of where their farm might have been, but saw nothing. He didn't think anything about it, as it was so dark that night.

Dean told the chaplain, "I looked at my watch and was shocked that it was only 3:15 a.m. How could all of that have taken only fifteen minutes?"

A couple of weeks later, Dean was on the same route. It was in the daylight, and this time, he had the front-end protector installed. He thought he would try to find the farm and again thank the two men that had helped him. He slowed down and watched very closely to see if he could spot the farm. There were no towns anywhere, nor did he see any farm buildings or signs of a farm within eyesight.

"How could the old man have been walking on the road, just when I needed him at 3:00 a.m.? And how could the son have gotten there so fast?"

Dean looked Mike in the eyes and quietly asked him, "Who do you think that was? They never told me their names, even though I had told them my name."

Dean spent another hour telling Mike about how the incident had changed him and strengthened his faith. He was now going to church services on a regular basis, and he was trying to help others whom he met. Mike told him that talking with him had strengthened his faith also. They said a prayer together and said good-bye.

8

ENGAGEMENT

(N o, we are not getting married.)
You might say that Mike didn't follow the
rules of engagement that we follow today. No, we're not
talking about the rules of warfare engagement. We're
talking about the rules of communicating with other
humans. Those rules say you should keep your distance
from other people, and you should not touch them.

Mike found that most people responded positively
to a friendly handshake. This probably freaks some
people out, that he went around touching other people's
hands with all the possible germs he could get. Eeeew!

As he was leaving, he would always say, "God Bless
you," and he would touch their shoulder or the top of
their head (if they were a child and only in front of their
parent of course). Some of you may feel, "Hey, you're
invading their personal space. Dude, that's not allowed!"
Mike would say to himself, "Bull!" He admitted there
had been two people in ten years that had backed away
from any touch, and he respected that.

Of course, with any personal contact, he had to be careful, but especially with truckers. He had to be careful not to infringe on their macho image. So he had to use some judgment as to whom it was that he was addressing and mindful whether or not they were pulling away from him or avoiding any contact at all.

He had found that people expected and welcomed him to shake their hand when he greeted them and to touch them when he gave them a blessing. People need closeness in their relationship with a minister of God and some of that includes appropriate touch. In these actions they felt closer to the minister and more willing to share their stories.

9

TURNED OFF

One night, Mike was going table-to-table as usual and met Isaiah who asked him,

"Sit and talk with me for a spell."

Isaiah was thirty-two years old and a very large individual; at least six foot eight inches tall and large in other ways, as he weighed well over 300 pounds. He had a kind, baby face and a slightly higher-pitched voice. This was kind of strange, but the man had endearing qualities.

He answered all of the usual introductory questions and was very friendly as Mike took his hand in both of his own when they shook hands. He started to talk about the fact that he was raised Catholic, but now attended another church. He changed because of a priest's attitude. Mike told him that was unfortunate, but a priest was only one human and did not represent the entire church. Mike could tell that this was an emotional subject and reached across the table to briefly touch Isaiah's hand.

"I live in a small town that had the only Catholic church for miles. So I had to find another church." Isaiah said.

Isaiah also explained how he felt about the Lord and other facts about his personal faith. Mike could tell that he was a very faith-filled man and all that he said seemed to be in line with standard Christian and Catholic beliefs.

Isaiah told Mike, "My current minister is very strict and won't let anyone wear jewelry, even wedding bands. The minister said that this is right out of scripture."

Isaiah continued, "This causes problems especially with the ladies getting hit upon by other men, when they don't wear wedding bands."

Mike said, "Isaiah, you said that you are involved in a Bible study group with the minister. Maybe you should bring up the problem with the group to look up the scripture involved and pray about it. Keep in mind that the scripture was written two thousand years ago, in a different language, for a culture we don't fully understand anymore."

A couple of weeks later, Isaiah was at the truck stop waiting for Mike. He couldn't wait to talk and came rushing over when Mike walked into the restaurant. He told him, "We need to talk!"

Mike was instantly worried and tried to remember what they had discussed the last time they met.

They sat down, and he proceeded to tell Mike, "I had the meeting with our Bible study group, and the Pastor said that they would pray over the question. The next week, they decided that you were right to question this practice and they will allow wedding rings to be worn. In addition, they will review some of their other practices in the same manner. The congregation was revitalized and on fire with the Sprit."

Mike and Isaiah talked for another hour and Isaiah told Mike about his family and the influence his mother had on his faith. As they parted, Mike said a prayer for the trucker and his family.

For a while, Mike saw Isaiah every week who talked about his new faith in action and how that was changing his life.

"I feel that to be a true Christian you have to be active and to help others, because the Holy Spirit is now within you," Isaiah said.

At some point Isaiah stopped coming to the truck stop and Mike even asked the waitresses to watch for him, but that was the last time he saw him. Even though he didn't see Isaiah any more, Mike felt they had a bond in faith that kept them together.

Isaiah said, "Thank you, Mike, for the faith in the Lord that we have shared. It will stay with me and be my strength forever."

Mike agreed with Isaiah, and many times found himself thinking of him, even after several years had passed, because his faith was so genuine and his desire to bring his faith into action was inspiring.

Mike told his wife later that night, "And who said, they are only truckers? Just think of the things they can teach us all. I am constantly amazed to find out how many of them have a deep faith in God."

10

THE JUDGE

Mike was sitting in his normal place at the restaurant counter. A man sat down next to him, wearing jeans, a black cowboy hat, and a denim shirt with torn-off sleeves and tattoos covering his entire arms. He also had a dark beard, which was not trimmed. Mike took a quick look and thought to himself, *I guess this will be a short conversation.*

Mike had told his wife, "I try not to judge others based on appearance, but I am only human." Another factor was that this happened at the counter, where it was rare to get into an in-depth discussion with anyone.

Fred sat next to Mike while he was eating, and Mike finally said hello to the man. Fred said in a low-key, "Hi," without looking at the Chaplain.

Mike finished his meal and decided to try for further conversation from Fred. So, he asked,

"Where are you from?"

"Nebraska."

"I'm the Chaplain here and just stopping by to say hello to everyone. What's your name?"

"Fred. What's yours?"

After they finished the introduction, he proceeded to tell Mike all about his family. Then he shared his ideas about his true beliefs and how he liked to play with his children and talk to them about the Lord.

Mike's mouth must have hung open for about a second. He was a little red-faced and had to admit to himself that he was astounded. They talked for about an hour, even though Fred's meal was getting cold in front of him. Mike even told him, "Please eat so your food won't get cold."

He replied, "I'd rather talk to you."

The discussion was very friendly and not pushy. They just shared with each other.

At the end of their conversation, Fred said, "I want to thank you for your support and for taking the time to listen and share your faith with me. It was like I was talking to my brother. I feel like I have gotten a shot of pure faith. Thank you and God bless you. Please keep doing this!"

Mike told Fred, "I also want to thank you for taking the time to share your faith with me. You have been an inspiration to me. You are the reason I started this ministry, because of people like you who take the time to share their deepest faith with me. It makes this ministry a two way relationship in the Lord's name."

Mike prayed on his way home that night to have the strength to not prejudge the people he would meet at the truck stop. He realized that these people were different than those he had met in his sheltered life, but they had just as much faith (if not more) than any people he had met before.

11

DISAPPOINTMENT

Mike walked up to a table and introduced himself with the normal questions. The young man was Tom and told Mike that he was twenty-five years old. He had a heavy Southern accent as he asked the chaplain to have a seat. Mike found Tom to be very friendly and high-spirited.

Mike noticed that many became drivers, because they felt that was all they could be. Tom was no exception to that sentiment.

He proceeded to tell the chaplain he was a driver with a weekly route from Ohio to Illinois, and a return to Ohio. He said, "It's not too exciting, but it pays the bills."

Tom told Mike about his mom and dad and the rest of his family that were very close to him. He also told him about the big old Victorian house he had bought last year and was trying to restore. They talked about this for quite some time, as Mike also liked doing woodworking projects and this one was really a challenge.

After some more of that conversation, Mike asked if Tom went to church. He said that he has started to go sometimes with his girlfriend. Tom said that he appreciated the fact that there was a chaplain at this truck stop and liked talking to Mike.

Mike saw Tom the next week and found that he had a set route, which meant he would be there every week. After the third week, he felt that they had attained a relationship of trust. He asked Tom why he only went to church sometimes. He thought for a moment and said, "I really don't know."

"Does your girlfriend like it when you go with her?"

"Yes, she does."

"Do you feel good about going with her?"

"Yes, now that you mention it."

"Maybe it would be good for both of you to go on a regular basis."

"You know, I think your right. I think I have just been too lazy to get up on Sundays, but I really want to go with her. Maybe it will help our relationship."

"I bet it would. At the very least; it can't hurt."

The following week, Tom told Mike that he had decided that going to church with his girlfriend was really good, now that he recognized the reasons to go, and it meant more to go with someone.

Mike asked him, "Why is that?"

He said, "Now that I am taking an active part in my faith and talking about it with my girlfriend, (and you) going to church has more meaning for both of us. And I like helping others. I feel like I want to help out."

Mike said a prayer for the both of them and gave Tom a blessing. He thanked Mike with a big smile on his face.

Mike saw Tom many more times over the next couple of months, and they shared many stories. Later, it was learned that his route had changed to a different day, and Mike's only contact was through the waitresses. Then Tom stopped coming to the truck stop all together.

Mike realized that it was one of the disappointments in this ministry that the people you meet were always on the move. You plant the seeds, but seldom get to see them grow and bear fruit, but when you do, it brings you such great joy; you feel like the Holy Spirit is lifting you up. Mike told his wife, "I know that may sound weird, but I don't know how else to explain the feeling."

12

WHAT IS THIS?

Mike was raised on a small farm near a little rural town in Illinois. And for eight years, he and his brothers attended a Catholic grade school, in another town ten miles from their home. A neighbor transported them to and from school every day.

He was a cradle-catholic who even contemplated becoming a priest for a short while. Of course, he thought his faith was the only faith, much like anyone born into a faith system, be it Catholic, Methodist, Lutheran, or whatever.

His mother had been raised Episcopalian but converted to Catholicism when she became engaged to her future husband. Mike's limited conversion experiences taught him that conversion occurred when a minister or priest asked or pushed someone to convert. He never thought about conversion of someone with no faith or someone with no knowledge of God. And of course he never thought about nurturing someone's existing faith. After all, you either had faith or you didn't, right? At least that's what he thought.

But Mike learned that in the real world, many of us have experienced pushy evangelization. Remember the door-to-door minister? What about the minister who asked, "Have you accepted Jesus Christ as your personal savior?" Or what about, "Have you been born-again?" Please don't misunderstand. I'm not saying that these evangelization styles are never effective, but, although well-intentioned, they sometimes tend to misuse the process and "turn-off" the would-be Christian or stop the conversion process. Mike met many people that said they had been saved, and it had changed their lives. They attended Sunday services, had started reading Scripture, and were trying to live the values contained in those pages. God Bless them!

Mike had encountered many others that had been pushed to the extreme, saying the prayers of salvation without any real faith, foundation or support. These people were like shell-shocked war survivors. At the very sight of a minister, they put up defenses or ran the other way. They were either quick to say, "Thanks, I've already been saved!" or they tried to head off any further conversation by saying, "I'm really tired." Sometimes of course, they may have even really *been* tired.

Mike had also personally met and talked with some who had been *saved*. They told him that they didn't need to do anything. Since they had accepted Jesus Christ and said the prayer, they were saved, no matter what they did. They could drink, run around with wild women, curse, rob a bank, or anything; they were already saved, and nothing could change that. They would say, "I'm not one of those do-gooders that try to do good things to earn salvation. That was a gift from Jesus, and it can't be taken away."

When they asked Mike if he had been saved, he would say, "Yes! Sometimes I have to be saved several times a day!"

He also told them that being saved was not a one-time act. It was a daily commitment, and because of this commitment and how it changed our hearts, we feel that we should change our lives and modify our actions to show what's in our heart and remain closer to God.

So, we try to not do all of those things that keep us away from God. We may struggle, but with the Lord's help, we try to act better than before. But, we are not doing good deeds to be saved; rather we do good deeds because our hearts are changed. After all, how much commitment can you have to the spirit of God living within you, if you believe you can continue with your bad habits after accepting God's gift? This can be likened to getting married and not having a commitment to your spouse.

"Yeah, I'm getting married then going on a fishing trip the next day with the boys for two weeks." Duh! What were you thinking?

Our relationship with God is not a private one. It's not just *me and God* as many people have said. It's also not just the *Lord as my personal savior*. We have a responsibility to have a close relationship with our family, friends, and all those we come in contact with each day.

13

THE CONVICT

Salvation is an unearned gift from God, through His son Jesus Christ, who died on the cross to give that gift to us. But like any gift, we can reject it, turn the other way, or stay in our own angry, little world. We all have free will. And we can say we accept the gift then do all of those things that take us way from the gift and God. Do we, therefore, really have the gift if we reject it?

A friend named Chuck told Mike a story about his jail ministry. Chuck had decided to give prisoners at the local jail a Mother's Day card that was stamped and all ready to be addressed and dropped in the mail. He had given a card to all the inmates who wanted them. He tried to spend time with each inmate that had requested the card to see if they had any concerns, and he left a few cards on a table for some of the more shy people.

The next week, he returned to find one of the inmates named Juan was very upset, so Chuck asked him what was wrong.

The man said, "I left it on the table, and someone took my card."

"So, why was the card lying around?"

"I decided not to send it, but it was mine."

Chuck tried to talk with the man, but Juan was in a hateful, angry state and was not willing to take another card or send it out.

This is an example of how we can get trapped by our own personal feelings and not be open to accept a gift, like the gift our Lord has given us in his gift of salvation.

Do you know anyone who is not accepting the gift?

14

SOW A SEED

C haplain Mike was asked to give a talk to a church group about his ministry to truckers. As part of his talk he said, "A major part of working with people in a religious or faith setting is to break through their defenses and the anger so that they can realize the gift of our Lord and accept it. Another problem with evangelization is that, without the relationship of other humans who are willing and are patient enough to nurture that newfound faith, it can whither and die, much like in Matthew's Gospel (Matt 13: 3-9):

> A farmer went out to plant some seed. As he scattered it across his field, some seeds fell along a footpath, and the birds came and ate them. Other seeds fell on shallow soil with underlying rock. The plants sprang up quickly, but they soon wilted beneath the hot sun and died because the roots had no nourishment in the shallow soil. Other seeds fell among thorns that shot up and choked out the tender blades.

But some seeds fell on fertile soil and produced a crop that was that was thirty, sixty, and even a hundred times as much as had been planted. Anyone who is willing to hear should listen and understand!

Jesus then explained the Parable of the Seed (Matt 13: 19-23):

The seed that fell on the hard path represents those who hear the Good News about the Kingdom and don't understand it. Then the evil one comes and snatches the seed away from their hearts. The rocky soil represents those who hear the message and receive it with joy. But like young plants in such soil, their roots don't go very deep. At first they get along fine, but they wilt as soon as they have problems or are persecuted because they believe the word. The thorny ground represents those who hear and accept the Good News, but all too quickly the message is crowded out by the cares of this life and the lure of wealth, so no crop is produced. The good soil represents the hearts of those who truly accept God's message and produce a huge harvest – thirty, sixty, or even a hundred times as much as had been planted.

This story from the Gospel of St. Mathew is a great beginning for us all. It gives us a basis for understanding the interface we have with the act of evangelization or change. We are there to nurture others faith, not convert them to a new faith. That nurturing is evangelizing.

So, at the truck stop, Mike knew he was evangelizing the people he met, but he was doing it one-on-one. And if you believe in your faith in God, you should always be evangelizing everyone you meet. An example is in Luke's Gospel of the lost sheep (Luke 15: 4–15: 7).

> If you had one hundred sheep, and one of them strayed away and was lost in the wilderness, wouldn't you leave the ninety-nine others to go and search for the lost one until you found it? And then you would joyfully carry it home on your shoulders. When you arrived, you would call together your friends and neighbors to rejoice with you because your lost sheep was found. In the same way, heaven will be happier over one lost sinner who returns to God than over ninety-nine others who are righteous and haven't strayed away!

What Jesus was saying was that we must take special care of those that need our help and attention most. Someone must leave the ninety-nine and go help the one that needs help. Go to them and nurture them."

Then Mike told them this story, "Because I was raised on a small farm, I had some farming and gardening experience. I knew that there were some other considerations for proper care of plants—and humans. Fertilizer can be a great help to plants in poor soil, but as a farmer, you have to know how and when to apply it. If it is given sparingly to the seedbed, the plants can thrive with the proper application of water, sunlight, and tilling to loosen the soil. This is a good example for the evangelizer. We must plant our seeds in the hearts of those we work with; then comes the real work as we carefully supply support, love, and care. You must foster their relationship with you, with God, and with others.

"If we as farmers, *blast* the plants with too much fertilizer, they will wilt and die as though they were suffering from a lack of water. This is also unique to each plant. Some can handle a lot, and others may dry up from the overload. The same is true for the people we work with. If we blast them with too much at the beginning of their faith journey, they will likely shrink away and maybe never come back. In addition, they may also develop a *Church-a-Phobia*, meaning that they put up immediate defenses at the sight or mention of a minister, church, or God.

"If we can get through their defenses and get them to share their true feelings of faith from the depths of their soul, we will find some incredible faith in the true God. All it takes is love and time. It is called a relationship."

15

THE GROUP

One night Mike was sitting at the front of the restaurant counter along with some other truckers all of whom looked to Mike like your typical drivers so he didn't expect much from the conversation. He was also eating, so he was sort of on-break. The truckers were telling stories of the road as they often do.

"Those d... four-wheelers. I almost crushed one of them today. They don't realize, or care, that we can't turn or stop like a car, yet they constantly cut us off or run up our blind spot even though we have our turn signal on. They will do anything and risk it all to get in front of us. How stupid can they be?" one of them said.

There was more conversation, then one of the truckers, named Will, from the other side of the U-shaped counter asked, "What do you think about that Rev.?"

Mike had to ask, "About what?" since he was not paying much attention to their conversation.

We all know that the Lord has a sense of humor. We find this especially true when we tell the Lord of *our plans*, then we find out that the Lord has different plans for us. In ministry we have to be keenly aware of the Lord's sense of humor when we think we have a situation all figured out or when we look at someone and think we have him or her figured. This is very true when we size someone up based on how they look. We all try not to do this pre-assessment but we are human. And the Lord often says, *surprise!*

Will repeated the question, "What do you think about the fact that most truckers don't go to church, because they have to travel on Sunday to get to their first delivery on Monday morning?"

Well, Mike was taken aback because of how he assessed the person asking the question. He would not have thought the man would be asking that kind of question. *Surprise!*

Mike pretended that he was swallowing a mouthful of food while he took a moment to privately apologize to the Lord.

Mike answered Will and said, "It depends on your faith or what you truly believe. Church is *not* the building; rather it is what's in your heart. The Lord said,

"For where two or three gather because they are mine, I am there among them. So, by your asking that question the Lord is here with us and this is church."

Will and the others were amazed and then, all of them said very loudly, "Amen!" like a cheer. The group continued in the discussion about faith and the Lord for a while, then, Mike went on his rounds of the tables happy that he was part of their church.

16

THE RELATIONSHIP

It is important as humans to be able to *read* people. That is, we must be able to sense what they are feeling. If they are leaning into our conversation, we can add more to the conversation. If they are leaning back, away from us, it could mean they are being cautious, getting overloaded with the subject or shutting down to what we are saying. It helps if we form a relationship with each person before we get into a heavy conversation about God or faith.

We are human, and as such, we were created to be in relationship with other humans and with God. We were also created to love each other, God, and ourselves (not necessarily in that order). This is as natural as saying that a bird was created to fly. However we, as humans, have free will and can choose not to love or be in relationship with each other and God. We can put ourselves in a corner away from everyone else. And like the bird when its wings are clipped for a long time, we can forget how to fly or to love.

We can get to the point in our lives where we have built up so much hate, despair, or other negative emotions, we forget how to love. All we see are the things that support those negative emotions. We say, "See, I knew that was going to happen!" And who do you think this really hurts? Negative feelings and anger usually hurts the one who is angry the most. Have you ever noticed that when you are angry for a long time, God is not part of the conversation? So, the anger takes us further from God and those around us. All of our relationships are damaged by the hatred we foster.

Hatred causes us to dwell on the negative. We push those we love away. God is also not part of our life, and our hatred deepens like a spiral. Of course, this leads to all kinds of emotional problems, like road-rage, divorce, or even suicide or murder. In good relationships, we try to work with others and treat them with respect and kindness.

In ministry Mike found that for many people the words they read or heard were not enough, even if those words were from the Bible. Many preachers never realize this limitation because they usually preach to hundreds of people at a time. It is part of our human condition, in which we need a relationship with one-on-one conversation and the touch of another caring person. This is not something weird or unacceptable. The touch can be a handshake, a tender touch on the arm, and a hug if they offer it, or some other form of affirmation and sharing of their pain or happiness.

17

DARKNESS WITHIN

M ike decided to leave the truck stop for the night. As he exited the building, he heard a familiar voice say, "Hey Rev."

It was Will, from the group discussion. He wanted to talk some more but did not want to talk about personal stuff in front of the other guys. This was a common occurrence for the Chaplain.

As Will approached, Mike was able to see the man's thin body and the weariness of the road on his face. Mike could also see a troubled look that went much deeper.

Will said, "I am very upset with how the world is going, and I pray that God will take me away. I had an accident a few months ago where I lost control of the truck I was driving, and it crashed into a guardrail, completely totaling the truck."

"The next thing I remembered was being up on a hill at the other side of the road, watching as the emergency workers put out the fire while they were looking for something. I thought I was dead. After a while a worker came up to where I was and asked me if I saw anyone get out of the truck."

Will said, "Yeah, I'm the driver."

The emergency worker looked at him in disbelief and said,

"Yeah, right! Whoever was driving *that* truck did not get out alive or is near death. You don't look like you have a scratch on you."

"I don't know how, but I'm the guy."

Will went to get up from a sitting position but fell over. The EMT helped him down from the hill and checked him for any injury. All he could find was a cut above his eye some bruises and weakness in his legs.

Will let Mike know he wished he had died in that crash. He was very negative toward others and said,

"I am so angry with how people treat each other. I would rather not be here any longer."

Mike told Will, "It is pretty clear that the Lord has a plan for you. You are meant to be here, and it shows in the fact that you survived that incredible crash. Do you believe that the Lord saved you?"

Will thought about it and said, "Yes. I guess so."

"As far as the problem you are having with the people you meet, maybe you could remember that the Lord saved you. You could also pick up on another idea. A trucker told me he has started to practice a positive attitude by simply, performing at least one *random act of kindness* each day on someone who is not being kind. That driver said it seems to be working, because he has experienced people who were mean and short-tempered with him in the past were now kinder and preferential toward him."

Will thought about it and said, "I guess I could try this random act of kindness thing." But then he said he needed to get back inside the restaurant before the other guys got suspicious (he didn't want them to know that he was talking to the chaplain about personal stuff.).

He thanked Mike and asked if the Chaplain could say a prayer for him.

Mike said a prayer for him, and they said goodbye.

A week later, Mike walked into the restaurant and one of the other drivers named Todd, who had been at the counter last week, came to Mike and pulled him to the side. He told Mike that he had noticed last week that Will was very negative. So, he talked with Will at the counter. After that they went out to the parking lot and talked for another hour and a half. He told Will that he needed to gain a more positive attitude himself, and that no one could do it for him. Todd also told Will that he tried to perform at least one random act of kindness each day. Will was surprised and said, "That's exactly what the chaplain told me. I guess I need to try it. I can't believe that you and the chaplain have taken the time to help me."

One of the problems in this ministry is that most of the driver's travel routes were random. And they never know where their company will send them next. Mike, therefore, had to assume he might never see the people he met, ever again. He could only give them his best shot. At least in this case he heard from another driver ho supported Mike and told Will the same thing.

Three months later, Mike was in the restaurant when a man came up to him and said with a big smile, "Chaplain, I don't know if you remember me. My name is Will. You helped me with a problem, and I just wanted to thank you. I tried the one random act of kindness, and it has worked so well that I do it all the time. God bless you!

18

FORCED

As a Truck Stop Chaplain, Mike ministered to those we would rather not see. At least that's what a minister's daughter from Minneapolis once told him, and that thought has stayed with him for many years now. It has been a ministry of presence to those people we all depend on and it has been one in which he didn't push or have an agenda or an overt need to *convert* them.

Many of the people we meet in our lives have been pushed and manipulated into things they didn't want. In other words, they have a need, but want to make up their own mind then make a commitment and do something about it in their own timeframe. They want to be invited, not pushed. And sometimes, because of their defenses, that invitation has to be very gentle, to be heard at all.

One night Mike was trying to explain to a trucker. He told the man, "Have you ever decided you needed a new car or worse yet, a used car? I'm sorry, to be politically incorrect, that's a pre-owned car. (Whatever!) So you go car shopping.

You do some homework as to the make and model you can afford that will give you the features you need. Armed with this key data (somewhat oblivious to the events that are about to unfold), you set off for the car dealership. You think that you should be able to make a great deal on the car of your dreams, or so you've been lead to believe. But, in the process, you encounter the infamous *car salesman*. And the salesman tries to steer you to a particular model and he explains why, "This is the perfect car for you." He may even give you a special price that's only good for today. Maybe you buy the car, but later you realize it is not what you wanted in the first place, especially since you were forced into the deal. Or maybe you decided to just forget it for now. Wow! How did *that* make you feel?

What about the expensive repair work on your home? The repairman tells you, "This is really necessary," but later, you find out it wasn't really necessary. How did you feel about being pushed into a decision you were not ready for? Now, imagine the situation is about religion, and someone is trying to tell you that you are going to Hell if you don't say you believe, right now.

We are human, and as humans we tend to be very independent. No one is going to tell us what to do. Independence is not inherently bad, but remember, we are human and need relationships to keep us sane and able to deal with others. Our independence seems to magnify when it comes to church, and it can get in the way of wise decisions.

The question of faith is also loaded with other baggage that we have carried along with us for years. We, therefore, have many emotions and feelings. One of those feelings is the guilt that we have acquired from many sources. There is also the longing, deep in our soul. And this is where the pushy minister sometimes makes headway with someone who is ready to be saved."

The driver thanked Mike for the example and for taking the time to explain.

19

SEEKING

T rue faith in God starts in our heart and develops a longing within our soul that should cause us to seek out a way to get closer to God in our lives. But for most people, this is a scary ordeal, and they need to do it on their own time or they won't be truly committed to the faith journey. In fact experience sometimes shows that instead of being brought closer to God, some of these people who were pushed actually get much farther from God, never to return. There have been examples of people who have refused to listen to words of faith (even on their death-bed).

So, it is apparent that many of the people we meet have been pressured into something at sometime in their lives. Someone who had a convincing way to get him or her to commit, used this pressure. How do you think they felt later? How did you feel about the car? Maybe the example of the car is not exactly the right allegory to religion and faith, but I hope you got the idea. The end result is that the victim feels animosity and anger and wants to reject any form of religion at the first sign of pushing from a minister.

Evangelization (bringing someone closer to God), like any good relationship, if it is to last, will take time to develop. Most of us would not think it a good idea to get married after knowing our potential spouse for only a couple of minutes. The relationship with the Almighty is even more complicated especially from the prospective of evangelization or change.

A very good friend of Mike's once said, "True ministry of evangelization has to include marketing." He also said, "In order to get people too church and be committed to sharing their gifts, you need to have a product that they can experience and want."

Mike realized that in ministry, he shouldn't have a quota unlike some of our contemporary Christians (or so it seems).

So, by not pushing, but spending time with each person and getting to know them and their needs, he can change them forever. By developing a personal relationship with them, he can form a need within them, to have what he has. Mike also gives them room to talk about what they really feel, especially when it comes to faith. Many of the truckers are ready and willing to talk about their own faith, once Mike gets past the idea and fears that he is there to push them into something.

Some of the fears expressed or hidden are: the fear that they will appear different, weird, and embarrassed. This is partly due to what they have seen from some of our Christian contemporaries. They also fear how being saved will affect their lives and what that commitment means to what they will be required to do, as a Christian. In other words, "If I become closer to God, will I have to pray a list of prayers every day?" "Will I have to wear a suit to church every Sunday?" He could see how their fears can start and grow.

20

THE DILEMMA

Mike met Terry from Maryland who was about twenty or twenty-five years old. He was a very likeable man with a bright, young, friendly face and short dark hair. He was cautious when he saw a chaplain walk up to his table. Then Mike explained that he was just there to say hello and talk if he wanted. Terry immediately asked the Chaplain to have a seat.

He talked first about the road, and then Mike asked, "Are you married?"

"No, I am single, but I have a girlfriend. We have been together for about a year now and I'm hopeful that things will develop into a lasting relationship."

"Do you get home on weekends?"

"Not always. I'm usually gone for two to three weeks at a time."

"Aren't you afraid that being gone that much will make your relationship with her difficult?"

"Yes, but I need to drive for a living."

"What about finding a different job?"

"I don't have any other skills, so another job would be a problem."

"What about getting a different driving job that would get you home more often?"

"That wouldn't work either, because those jobs don't pay as much."

They talked about that and other things for another ten to fifteen minutes, but it was clear that he was not about to consider any other job other than the one he had. Mike could sense a darkness within the man. It seemed like a trap that could doom him and his relationship with his girlfriend, so Mike changed the subject for the moment.

He told him, "Our ministry is a little different, because we don't push. We talk like normal human beings and mostly listen. We discuss whatever you want to talk about, but we may ask questions about your life and your needs."

"That's incredibly good, because I also have experienced pushy preachers and a pushy mom. Oh, I love her dearly, but I need to do this God thing in my own time and on my own schedule."

He said that he was raised Amish with all of their strict ways. And he has been unhappy with the church he sometimes attended, because, "They put on airs. Meaning that everyone would dress up in suits and ties, and that seemed to be the most important part of their "Sunday-go-to-meeting time."

He said, "Why can't churches be more open to people and accept them as they are?"

Mike told him, "In fact, we are at church right now, as we talk about God and our relationship with him. Because, Jesus had said, 'For where two or three are gathered together because they are mine, I am there among them.' But Terry, you need to find a church that accepts you and nurtures you."

Terry said that after some shopping around, he had found a church where he felt welcome at his own level. He went there with his girlfriend when he could.

Mike told him about the Thomas Merton prayer card that he had adopted as the Trucker's Prayer, especially the part, 'Lord I don't know where I am going. I do not see the road ahead of me.' It sounded like it was only for truckers or for someone who shouldn't be giving directions, but it was for all of us who might think, *I know where I am going.*

Mike asked him, "So, do you think we really need to look to the Lord for our direction?" Terry agreed.

He asked if Terry would like to have one of the prayer cards.

Mike told him, "Many truckers keep the card on the dash of their truck to pray when they need it."

He read the first part, and said' "Yes, please."

Terry thanked Mike and said, "I really liked talking to you. This is the kind of ministry we need more in churches as well as on the road."

They talked some more about his faith then said goodbye. As Mike was leaving, he looked back and saw Terry reading the card.

This was another example of how both of them got an incredible boost of faith, in the actions and words of a nurturing relationship with another person and God. Mike planted some seeds about Terry's relationship with his girlfriend and with God. He also planted a seed in the form of a question about his job. Mike knew that he might never see Terry again.

Mike just said, "I leave it up to you, Lord. Let's see what grows."

21

AFFIRMATION

Mike was convinced that truly great ministry happens when both sides gain something from the experience. It's the same in our personal relationships. It's give and take. It's not very fulfilling if it's always you giving or you taking. As married couples we learn this many times in our life together as we give and take, in a spirit of love.

The Gospel of Mathew, (Matt 8: 5-8) is an evangelization story in which Jesus shows his excitement when a Roman officer begged Jesus to heal his faithful servant.

Jesus says, *"I will come and heal him."*

The officer was quick to say, *"Lord, I am not worthy to have you come into my home. Just say the word from where you are, and my servant will be healed!"*

Jesus forms a relationship with this pagan soldier who shows his true belief and Jesus affirms that belief by saying, *"I haven't seen faith like this in all the land of Israel!"*

And so it is in our lives, relationships are a key to an evangelizing roll. You might be saying right now, "Hey, I am not in an evangelizing roll in the church." Weeeeelllll! I've a news flash for you! If you really believe in God and your church, you should always be in an evangelizing roll.

Do you know what makes someone in sales or marketing successful? It is believing in their products so much that they are always talking and acting as a believer and inviting others into the realm of their products. Not by beating them over the head, but by inviting them into a meaningful conversation and asking them questions about their situation and their life. Get them to want what you have. This is the way to get them to be a believer in your church products as well, and they will be firm in their belief in God, because it was really their idea that you affirmed.

But, always be careful that you don't over-feed your products to the people you meet and turn them off.

22

WHO ARE YOU?

Mike saw a man around five foot tall come in and sit next to him at the counter. The Man was about fifty years old and looked so tired that Mike did not think he would want to talk. By now in his ministry, Mike had learned to not even notice what the drivers wore, after all, how they looked didn't mean anything anyway. Mike started by making some comment about the beautiful day, and the man agreed.

Mike asked, "Where are you from?"

"Virginia."

"What's your name?"

"Quinn."

"Are you married?"

Mike noticed a strange look on Quinn's face as he answered, "No. Divorced."

Then Mike realized that he had not introduced himself, and he quickly said, "I am the chaplain here."

Mike saw him immediately relax.

He said, "I'm glad you said that, because my next words would have been, 'And who the hell are you to be asking me all those questions?'"

They both laughed.

He told Mike, "Drivers need to be very careful with the information they give to strangers these days. There is a large increase in hijacking of trucks. Call it the economy or land pirates, but the value of the cargo is very tempting to those thieves."

Mike told him about the ministry, and he proceeded to tell Mike how his ex-wife surprised him with her boyfriend. He also told Mike about his two boys, and they talked about that for a while.

Quinn became very open to talking (once he knew who was asking the questions). They talked about his life and the difficulty of being on the road all the time.

He owned his own rig and knew (down to the penny) how much it cost to run each mile.

To change the subject, Mike asked him if he had a church back home, and he said not really; he had not been a churchgoer since he had a run-in with a pastor.

Mike said, "I'm sorry that happened, but pastors are just people, and I have met some very dumb pastors."

Mike told him, "I like to talk to the Lord while I'm driving instead of formal prayer. Because, it's like talking to my brother about what's happening in my life, and I get the help I need to get throughout the day."

Mike could see that Quinn was a little nervous about that. So, he decided to let it sink in while he changed the subject, and they talked for a while longer. Even though Quinn was tired, he was smiling when they parted and so was Mike. As Mike left him, he said, "God Bless you." Quinn thanked Mike for talking to him.

Faith is something to be shared. Quinn was not ready to accept the full message, but Mike planted a seed. He also decided that it was time to say good-bye and let the seed grow.

Sometimes more is not better, just like the fertilizer. If we give too much, instead of nurturing, it chokes.

23

DENIAL

(Not just a river in Egypt.)

Mike met Bert from Alabama. Actually, as Mike was stepping into the hallway to exit the restaurant, Bert called out loudly across the room, "Reverend!"

The Chaplain didn't catch it at first, and Bert hollered again, only louder this time, "Reverend!"

He heard it that time and turned to see Bert motioning for him to come over. The man was quite large and had a full light-brown beard. With sadness in his voice, he asked Mike to sit down. Mike could see the man was suffering with a heavy burden as he proceeded to tell the Chaplain that his brother, Ron, was dying. Then Bert told Mike, "I lost my wife five years ago to liver cancer. Now, my older brother was told that he has a blood disease that can't be treated, and he has only a month or so to live. I don't know what to do. My brother and I have been very close, but now he won't even talk to the minister that the family sent. That minister was one of the nicer ones around."

Mike said, "Maybe he is in denial or has had a bad experience with a minister."

He also told Bert, "A close friend of mine named Kirk was a church-going person, but refused any prayers at his deathbed. We tried many approaches, but all were turned away. It really hurt that we were not able to help Kirk in his final hours with a prayer service. So, we decided to just be present and spent time with him by having someone with him twenty-four, seven. We also prayed for him in church and silently at his side."

Mike talked with Bert for some time about his wife, and then they talked about his dying brother Ron.

To lighten it up, he told Bert the humorous story about the Merton prayer card and how it had helped many other drivers.

Mike told Bert, "A few months ago, I was planning to have a meeting of the Truck Stop Chaplains at my house. I decided to send an e-mail with directions, but wanted to include a short prayer. I found a prayer by theologian Thomas Merton that seemed appropriate.

"Well, some people called me, kind of snickering and asking, 'Was that meant to be a joke? Your e-mail said, *My Lord God, I have no idea where I am going. I do not see the road ahead of me. Here are the directions to my house.*' I laughed and told them that I had not really pictured it that way, but I could see the humor."

Mike suggested that Bert talk to his brother and tell him about the chaplain and the funny story about the prayer card to see if Ron would let him read the prayer to him as a starter. He said he would try it.

Mike said a prayer for Bert who had red, tear-stained eyes, Bert said good-bye, and he thanked Mike for taking time with him.

"It means so much to me that I can't even begin to describe it to you," he said.

As they parted, Mike knew that he had answered a prayer that evening.

24

RETIRING

A smiling man with new jeans and a clean, brightly colored short-sleeved shirt was sitting at the counter when Mike walked into the restaurant. Mike recognized the man, but didn't remember his name. Terry was gracious enough to tell Mike his name and saved the Chaplain's embarrassment. He was very excited to tell Mike, "I am retiring tomorrow!"

Mike was happy for him, and they talked about his situation, as he had not seen Terry for months. He got divorced when his wife of twenty-three years left him, three years ago. Terry also told Mike that his son had committed suicide about the same time.

Mike asked him, "How are you doing with all of that? I know that the pain does not go away."

He said, "You're right! But, I am handling it. I still miss my son terribly, but I have gotten closer to my faith in God, because I know my son is with Him and that has helped me."

"I have recently signed-up with a Christian dating service. It cost nine hundred dollars to join, but they set me up with six Christian dates a month, for a year. And if I do not meet *the one* in that year I get another year free. The service says they have a ninety-five percent success rate in the first year."

Mike didn't say anything, because he didn't pretend to know anything about dating services, but that sounded really expensive to him.

"All I want is to meet someone who will love me, and we can live our lives together in a loving relationship."

They talked some more and he asked Mike, "Have you sold your house yet?"

"No, but I am hopeful."

"How is the truck stop ministry going?"

"Well, I used to have someone here each weekday night, but they have all moved on. Why? Are you interested?"

"I might be. I will pray about it and call you on Tuesday to let you know."

Mike didn't know if Terry would help or even if he would call back. Mike did know that Terry left the truck stop that night with high expectations as he thanked Mike for being there for him. The Chaplain told him, "I will pray for you and your retirement."

Mike never heard back from Terry, but he realized that most people were reluctant to give a phone number or call back, to a relative stranger, for anything.

25

DELAYED

Mike met Robert from Atlanta who was forty-five years old and had been married for eighteen years and had been driving for just one year. His wife Gina normally came with him, but he was on his own for this trip. They decided eighteen years ago to delay having kids, but sadly never got around to having them. He told Mike that he wished that they had had kids. As he got older, he realized that fact more and more. He told mike stories of being with his brother's children and how much he loved them. He said he was now forty-eight years old and his wife was too old to have children. "Maybe you could still adopt", Mike told him.

"That would be great," Robert agreed.

"I think you should talk to your wife, and the two of you can pray about it."

Robert also told Mike, "I had a good job until a year ago when I got laid off. There were no other jobs around, so I decided to become a truck driver. I signed up for the truck driver school and completed my on-the-road portion of the practical training.

Within a couple of months, I got a raise to thirty cents a mile, but it was hard to make any real money with all of the laws, the traffic, and the rules. I guess we were so busy living our lives, we just didn't make time to sit down and discuss when we should have children. We have had some difficult times with the economy and everything, but we should have decided long ago to have children."

They talked for a long time about children, and Mike could see how much Robert loved them. They also talked quite a bit about the possibility of adoption.

"I will call my wife tonight and see if we can find out about adoption" he told Mike.

Mike said the following prayer for Robert and his wife, "Father, please bless my friends Robert and his wife. Lord, show them a new revelation of Your love and power. Oh Holy Spirit, please minister to their spirit and help them with their decision. Amen."

Robert was very happy and reached across to grab and hold Mike's hand as he thanked him several times. Just then, Robert's cell phone rang, and it was his wife. Mike could hear as he walked away, "Hi Gina. I am talking to the Chaplain here at the truck stop, and he had an excellent idea…"

26

THE ATHEIST

As Mike sat at the restaurant counter waiting for a reporter from the local newspaper, Joseph came and sat two seats away. Mike said hello, and the man returned the greeting. Mike told him that he was the truck stop chaplain just stopping by to say hello. He asked the man's name. He gave Mike his name and looking directly into the Chaplain's eyes, he said, "I'm an atheist." Mike looked back into the man's eyes and kind of nonchalantly said, "Okay."

Mike paused, then asked, "Are you married?"

Joseph seemed surprised and said, "I'm divorced."

"How long have you been divorced?"

"Two years."

"Do you have children?"

"I have two boys that are all grown up."

Mike could see from his look that Joseph was completely taken aback by this approach. He thoroughly expected the Chaplain to make some religious comment about his atheism statement. He told Mike that even his brother jumped all over him when he confided that he was an atheist. But he then proceeded to tell Mike all about his boys and his ex-wife.

Most truckers travel on somewhat of a scheduled route. Some are day drivers and are home most nights. Others have a schedule that gets them home each weekend. Some get home only once every two to three weeks. Still others are out for one, two or three months at a time. It makes for a very lonely life and one that makes a lasting married life impossible for all but a rare few.

Mike asked Joseph how often he got home.

He said, "I have not been home for two years, after she walked out on me."

"What about your boys? Don't you get to see them?"

"I have not seen them for the last two years.

"Do you ever talk to them on the phone?

"Sure, I talk to them all the time on the phone. In fact, even though I haven't been there, one of my boys lives in my house."

This meeting happened the week before the Fourth of July. So, Mike told Joseph that he should take the Fourth of July off and go home to surprise his boys. Joseph thought this was a wonderful idea, and he was going to take the entire week off. Joseph was so excited, and it showed as a great smile on his face.

The reporter Mike had been waiting for showed up, and it was time to say good-bye. So, he asked Joseph if he could give him a blessing. Joseph looked into Mike's eyes again for a moment, and then said, "I'll accept it from you!"

Mike gave him a short blessing and said, "God bless and keep you safe on the road. Lord, bless Joseph and his boys and make the time they have together loving and healing."

The reporter Mike was meeting wanted to write an article for a local newspaper about the truck stop ministry. So she wanted to get pictures of Mike ministering to a trucker. He went over to Joseph and explained about the reporter's needs and asked, "Would you allow the reporter to take pictures of me ministering to you." To Mike's surprise, Joseph said yes.

When all of the activities with the reporter were completed, Mike decided to take a break outside with the truck stop manager. While they were talking, Joseph came out and walked around them, then proceeded to lean against a post near them. Mike went over to Joseph, who looked at the Chaplain with a happy smile. He wanted to thank Mike for not jumping on him about being an artiest.

He said, "If you had, I would have ended the conversation right there. I also wanted to thank you for the encouragement to go home to see my boys. I decided to call them so we could make plans. They were very happy and were planning a welcome home party."

Mike told Joseph the humorous story about the Thomas Merton prayer card and gave him the card and asked him to read the first two lines and told him, "Now, remember, this was on an e-mail of directions to my house."

Joseph read it and laughed as he said, "My Lord God, I have no idea where I am going. I do not see the road ahead of me."

Mike told him, "You can have the card, and you can keep it or discard it. Many drivers like to keep it in their truck at all times." Joseph took the time to read the rest of the card and said he would keep it.

Mike asked him, "Please get back to me the next time you are here and let me know how it went with your sons."

He said he would. Mike later heard that the meeting had gone well. He also knew that he had planted more than one seed in Joseph's heart, which was now filled with good and fertile ground.

27

THE REPAIR

Mike walked up to the booth where Trent was eating his dinner. It had been an extremely hot and humid day. So, that evening, most truckers had the fatigue of the road etched into their faces as they came into the truck stop, and Trent was no exception. After the introduction and a few questions about his family, he invited Mike to have a seat.

Trent told Mike he was from Idaho and traveled to Chicago on a weekly basis then back to Idaho, but lately he had been struggling because business was down. He told Mike all about his wife, three children, and his new granddaughter. Then he shared his dilemmas with the Chaplain.

He said he owned his own truck, but he recently lost a large contract because his truck broke down and was in the shop for three weeks. It seemed his truck had blown the transmission and would cost $20,000 to repair. Needless to say, he did not have that kind of money to get it fixed. He finally put the charge on his credit card with the hope that he could quickly pay it off once the truck was repaired.

Trent also told me that his wife hated her job, which paid very little, and her boss treated her and others badly. He said that things were getting worse between him and his wife and feared that they were headed for divorce.

He then started to share his faith and beliefs. He was a church-going man and just before Mike walked up to his table, he was praying that God would send some help. So he was a little surprised when the Chaplain showed up at that moment. Mike said a prayer and gave him the Thomas Merton prayer card. He read it and said thank you. He also told Mike that this kind of ministry was different and very much needed. Mike told him that many people asked "Do you hold services or do you have a chapel at the truck stop? I tell them no, but someone two thousand years ago used to spend a lot of time among the people, so we figured we should do the same."

Trent said, "It seems your ministry is working. Keep doing it."

A couple of months later, Mike saw Trent at the truck stop again. This time he was very happy to see the Chaplain and invited him over to his table to be seated.

He told Mike, "There is much for us to discuss, and you won't believe all that has happened since the last time we met."

Trent told Mike that he had used the Thomas Merton prayer so much that he wore it out, but he had gotten three copies from Mike.

When he got home, he and his wife started to talk about their dilemmas with no solutions at hand. He decided to tell her of meeting the Chaplain, right after praying for help. Then he put the prayer card on the table for her to read it. After she read it, she agreed and said that they should say the prayer each day.

Within a couple of weeks, he had a new client and was making good money. He had since paid off the repair bill on his truck. His wife got a better job closer to home for double the money, working for a great boss. Trent was also now very happy with his relationship with his wife and said he would keep saying the Thomas Merton prayer every day. He said, "Isn't it amazing how things can change in your life with a little faith in the Lord?"

28

SUPPORT

Sometimes, the faith of those we serve is as strong or stronger than our own faith. Then we might ask ourselves, 'Who is ministering to whom?' And, if we can be rooted in the Lord, it's okay, because we are growing and so are they.

Michael met with a happy looking man named Ken from Upper Michigan. Ken was a devout born-again Christian. He was committed to the Lord, but was not pushy about it. He talked about his family and his faith. Both men shared their ideas and concepts on an extremely friendly basis. They talked and talked and never got tired. As each would share some thought the other would listen and only give words of support, encouragement, or to give an example or additional info. Michael had to admit later that it was like talking to the Lord himself.

Mike finally looked at his watch and discovered that they had been talking and listening for two hours. Then they talked for a while more. Michael said a prayer, and Ken added more to the prayer.

As they said their good-byes, Ken said, "Mike, this has not been a meeting of two people."

(Ken paused and Mike wondered where this was going.) Ken continued, "This has been a meeting of two souls. I feel like I have just been talking to the Lord himself. I have never had a conversation like this in my life. You asked me questions and listened to my answers and responded in a way that supported my faith like never before. Wow! You have to keep doing this."

Mike agreed with him and told him, "You have ministered to me as much as I have to you. You are one of the reasons I started doing this ministry. The Lord and the Holy Spirit were truly with us this evening."

Mike thanked Ken for his time and gave him a blessing.

Mike told his wife when he got home that night, "Sometimes, we are there to help them tell their stories. Sometimes, we are there to nurture and boost their faith. In some of those instances, we can do both. It is at those times when we nourish them the most."

29

REJECTED

Mike met a trucker named Lance from Colorado, who told him he had been married for thirty-three years and had three children, two boys and a girl. All of them were grown and married.

He also told Mike, "I have two brothers and two sisters, and we inherited our father's three thousand acre farm. One of my brothers runs the farm, but I make the deals to sell the farms products, and one of my sisters does the bookkeeping and the other runs the livestock ranch."

"My family is quite well off, but I drive a truck to have an income of my own for my family. I don't like living off of the money we make from the farm. Instead, I invested it and will use it for retirement and charity."

"When my children went to college, I made them pay their own way. When the kids found out how rich we really were, they were very upset at first and asked, 'Why did you do that to us?' I wanted them to develop character and gain from the experience. Later, after they were on their own, they each agreed with me."

He then asked Mike, "How do we get saved?"

Mike said, "What do you think?"

Lance said without hesitation, "I guess we are saved by accepting Jesus into our heart as the one who provided the forgiveness to save us.

"Yes. But is there anything that can affect that?"

He thought about it, then said, "I suppose, like any gift, we could refuse it, or we could reject it after we have said we accept it."

"Lance, you could not have been more correct."

They talked for another hour or more, and Mike learned that Lance was very happy with his life. He had enough money to live on from his driving activities. He had saved up for his retirement and now had sufficient funds to be able to help his children and others in need.

As he talked about how good his life had been, he realized that he needed to give thanks to God for all He had done for him. Lance looked at the Chaplain and said in a low voice, "Could we say a prayer?"

Lance started with, "Thank you, dear Lord for all you have given me and help me to remember and share your love with others."

Mike continued, "Lord, keep the Holy Spirit with Lance and his entire family and help them to always be kind and charitable to each other and to others in need."

30

MARRIED

Ron rushed in with clothes that smelled of diesel fuel. He came to sit at the counter next to Mike. The Chaplain did the usual introduction and asked the man's name. Then, Mike asked, "How long have you been driving?"

"Forty-one years." Ron seemed distracted as he answered.

"You must have quite a few miles."

"I quit counting after three million."

"Do you get home on weekends?"

"I get home every weekend."

"Are you married?"

Mike was confident he already knew the answer. Ron said, "Yes, for forty-one years, which is two weeks longer than I have been driving."

Mike smiled and said, "I have learned that drivers who get home on weekends to nurture their family relationships usually are married for many years."

"It doesn't take rocket science to figure that out," Ron said with a smile.

They both laughed, but Mike was well aware that it was no laughing matter. It was a serious problem for drivers and their families. They have one of the highest divorce rates in the country.

"I have to call in to get my next load," Ron said as he picked up his cell phone.

Mike realized that Ron really didn't want to talk, or was just rushed. So, he quietly said, "God bless you." As he touched the man's shoulder, Ron turned and mouthed, "Thanks," and Mike moved on.

31

TO DRIVE OR NOT TO DRIVE

Tom was a very young man in his twenties who looked like he hadn't a care in the world. After the introduction, he told the Chaplain he needed to talk about a marriage problem.

He said, "My wife wants me to quit my job and be home each night with her. I would also very much like to be home each night, but I can't make this kind of money if I do that. My wife and I are fighting about this all of the time. So, I'm stuck. I don't know what to do."

Mike asked, "Are you a praying man?"

Tom looked at him kind of surprised; then he looked down and softly said, "I pray once in a while."

"Well, I have an idea, if you don't mind?"

"Sure! Any idea at this point would be welcome."

"Maybe you could arrange to meet with your wife and talk this over in a loving discussion. Look at the problem with real data of how much money you really need to pay the bills. Maybe some bills will be less or not-needed if you work closer to home. Then, both of you should pray for guidance from the Lord. I am no expert, but I do know that you can find a workable solution with this strategy."

Tom thanked Mike and said he would try the Chaplain's approach.

Later that same night, Tom excitedly came up to Mike and said, "I called my wife to tell her what you said. I also told her that I wanted to talk seriously and lovingly with her about my job. She said, 'That's a great idea. I will make a special dinner for just the two of us and we can talk.'"

Tom was very happy at the prospect of talking with his wife to see what they could work out.

Mike said a prayer with Tom and said good-bye, knowing that he had helped a couple toward a solution.

Mike later told his wife, "Most drivers are not willing to risk their job to see if they can get home on weekends. They know that they have to be away from home and put on miles to make the money the family needs to survive. It's a catch-22. You want to be home with the family and wife, but the only way you know how to make money is to keep driving and away from those you love and need."

"In other cases, some drivers like the freedom of being on their own, on the road. In some cases, this was an avoidance of responsibility. So, if he wanted to stay up late, talking to the boys at the truck stop or do some things he would not be able to do at home, he was free to do them on the road.

In any case the result was usually the same—the wife got tired of always being alone and eventually found someone else. The divorce rate among truckers was, therefore, very high. Mike was told that it was as high as sixty percent."

32

GIVEBACK

Sitting next to the Chaplain, Jim was a rather hardened looking man with a deep voice and a face that told a story of a tough life, but to Mike's surprise, Jim said he wanted to talk about his faith. He told Mike he has had some things happen in his life that stirred his faith and now he wanted to giveback for all God had given him.

Mike asked him what had happened and how his faith has been strengthened. Jim spent the next forty-five minutes sharing with the Chaplain about his faith and his story.

He said, "I had a heart attack, and the doctors didn't think I would make it. They said they couldn't operate till there was some improvement because I also had a serious infection. My wife brought in the entire family around my bedside, and they decided to pray for me. I was under medication that kept me out. As I was drifting in and out of drug-induced sleep, somehow I became aware that my family was there for me, and I heard them praying, and I remember feeling a strange warm glow come over me.

"It could have been due to the drug, but the next day, I was so much improved that the doctors took me off of the heavy medications. They decided to operate on me that afternoon for a quadruple by-pass.

"In addition, I had no health insurance. I didn't know how I would be able to pay for the hospital stay and the operation. My wife and I prayed together that night. She also asked the church congregation to pray for me.

"The doctors wanted to study my case, because of my surprising recovery, so they decided to reverse most of their bill. Also, the church that my wife attended took up a collection and paid almost all of the rest of the bill.

Jim said, "I know that the Lord was at my side in the hospital, when everyone prayed for me. I never would have made it otherwise. And I definitely know the Lord helped make the bills go away."

They talked about what he planned to do to giveback.

He said, "I plan to give some money to our church for others in need and spend some time helping out."

Jim also realized that it would be difficult, since he was on the road so much.

Mike said, "You could try to help others at each truck stop. One way is to talk to other truckers and tell them how you have been helped and how you now want to help others. Then ask them questions about their families and their lives, but be careful, proceed with caution, drivers may not see the goodness of your intentions and be willing to share their personal information."

Jim understood. He said, "I will tread lightly at first till I get a feel for how to do it."

He thanked Mike and asked the Chaplain to pray with him. They prayed, and Mike gave him a blessing. Then Mike told him, "God has already blessed you, but when you recognize those blessings and thank the Lord, the Lord will give you even more."

Jim said, "I am extremely happy that I met you. You have been the answer to a prayer. I feel like I am floating three feet off the ground on a cushion of faith. Thank you! And God Bless you for your ministry and for being here for me."

33

OTHER PROBLEMS

Mike had countless conversations with men about how much they missed their wives and how difficult trucking was on their marriages and their kids.

Mike also had many conversations with men about their faith in God and how much this new ministry to the traveler was needed, especially for the truckers.

One driver said, "You know that we can talk to other drivers at the counter about the road, but it is difficult to talk about your family or your faith. Some ministers are so darn pushy. With you, I feel like I can talk about anything. You are like family. You have to keep doing this. We need you more than you know."

Another subject that was common with most drivers was about money problems.

One driver named Oliver said to Mike, "I just don't know how much longer I can keep driving and losing money. I own my rig and the cost of fuel and repairs is just too much."

Mike talked with the man some more and asked him, "Tell me something, if you wouldn't mind? How much do you make in a year?

Oliver sat up and proudly said, "Last year I made seventy-five thousand dollars."

"That sounds like a lot of personal income to be almost broke."

"Well, I have a lot of expenses."

"What kind of expenses?"

"Well, there's the truck payment"

"How much is your truck payment?"

"Two-thousand one-hundred and fifty dollars a month."

After they went through as many expense items as they could recall, Mike discovered that the seventy-five thousand dollars was the gross income for Oliver's company, before expenses. After adding the expenses up, they subtracted them from his gross income.

Mike showed him that he was only making about twenty-five thousand in personal income, before taxes.

"That's barely a poverty level of income. You need to reduce expenses and get more income per mile. You can't accept loads that only pay one dollar a mile, or you will go broke."

Oliver had never looked at his income that way before. He always thought he was making seventy-five thousand dollars a year.

Mike told him, "Most drivers know, down to the penny, how much it costs, including profit, to move their rig per mile. The profit in this case is the money your family has to live on."

He thanked the Chaplain, and told him that he would work on this new plan. He asked Mike to say a prayer for him and his family.

34

THE SURVIVOR

Ron was a normal looking driver with a friendly face. He told Mike, "Hello, chaplain. Believe it or not, you're looking at a man that has had cancer since 1979."

"I had part of my liver removed. I got over that and was doing better when they discovered that I had more cancer in my kidney, which had to be removed.

"That took me down for a while, and they felt they had gotten all of the cancer. Things were going well again until they found cancer in one lung, which also had to be removed. Even though that took even longer for me to recover, I'm still walkin' and talkin' and fightin' for my life. It has now been two years that I have been cancer free."

Mike told him, "I had cancer of the throat twelve years ago. And like me, you are a light for all to see, because you have survived. You must not give up hope after all this time, because God has a plan for you."

Mike asked Ron to write to him. This made Ron very happy that a chaplain like Mike would take the time to talk to him in a place like this. He said, "Dear Lord, please bless Michael as our chaplain."

Ron did write to Mike and let him know that he was still cancer free.

35

NOT MARRIED

Mike talked to Janice who worked at a local fast food restaurant. She was very young at twenty-one years old and quite pretty with long blond hair and a slender figure. She told Mike that she liked to stop in for a cup of coffee to relax for a minute before heading home.

"I have two children with the man I am living with. We're not married, but I wanted to have my children before I get too old."

That statement took Mike's breath away for a moment, but he recovered enough to ask, "Is he planning to marry you?"

She was surprised and looked at him funny, as if to say, *why are you asking me that?*

Mike was surprised himself that he jumped right out there with such a heavy question without knowing much about her situation. There didn't seem to be any real harm however, as she said, "I hope so."

A couple of weeks later, Janice appeared happy and excited to see Mike.

"I was thinking over what we talked about," she said.

"So, I had a loving talk with my boyfriend, and we decided that we should get married next month."

Mike congratulated her. Then he saw the light in her eyes fade and said, "I sense there is something wrong."

She told him, "I am upset that my pastor said, 'I will not marry you because, you have had children out-of-wedlock.'"

"Then maybe you should ask him for the name of another pastor who will be able to marry you and help you become an honest woman."

"That sounds like a good idea"

The following week, Janice was even more excited because she had talked to her pastor and told him what the Chaplain had said.

She told Mike, "The pastor agreed that my chaplain was right to say that he should be helping me. So, we have worked out the differences, and he will marry us in our church. I'm so excited I could scream!"

Mike was amazed and happy for Janice as she gave him a big hug. Each week she gave Mike an update on the wedding plans. Several weeks after the wedding, she described a blow-by-blow description of the wedding and reception. It all sounded so wonderful.

36

CHRISTMAS

Each week Mike would talk to Janice and hear about how she was doing. But, months after the marriage and the celebration, he heard that things were not going well. Mike tried to intervene but could not get a clear picture of what was wrong. Then the husband left, and they got a divorce.

The situation was dire. She had three small children, working at a restaurant, with Christmas coming in only a month. So, Mike found out the ages of the children and submitted them to his church's Christmas Drive. They came up with many presents for the kids, their mom, as well as some gift cards for the family.

He brought them out to the truck stop one evening, a couple of weeks before Christmas, and went in to get Janice. He told her, "Please come with me."

"Why? Where are we going?"

"It won't take long. But you will need your coat."

It was snowing and quite cold with a strong breeze blowing out of the east. They went out to his SUV, which was loaded with gifts and he opened the back and told her, "These are all for your kids."

He handed her the envelopes with gift cards for local stores,

"And these are for you to help out with Christmas."

She couldn't believe it and started crying as she gave him a big hug. As they went back into the restaurant, she thanked him and said, "I'll get a friend with an SUV to transfer the presents. The kids are really going to be overjoyed this Christmas. I didn't think I would be able to get much for them this year with all that has happened. How did you do this?"

"My church made it happen? They are people of God who really care."

She gave him another hug and said, "God Bless you and your church. It's amazing that someone really does care. Maybe God answered my prayer."

37

GRANDFATHER

Cynthia was a forty-five-year-old driver from Iowa.
She supported her un-married daughter and her
daughter's child. She was one of the few female drivers
that Mike had met.

Cynthia told him the story of her vision in the garden.

"When I was only ten years old I was kind of a loaner
and used to play in my parents back yard all the time.
This one day, however, I went walking to see grandpa's
old house. As I was walking down the street about three
blocks from our home, (almost at grandpa's house) a car
pulled up and my father jumped out and scolded me for
leaving the yard without telling anyone I was leaving."

"Dad took me home and asked,
'Where were you going anyway?'"

"To grandpa's house."

"'How would you even know where that was?
Grandpa has been dead for 9 years. Who told you
where it was?'"

"The old man I met in the vegetable garden."

"'What old man? You know you are not supposed to talk to strangers.'"

"Well he said that I should go to see his old house. It's just three blocks down and one to the left."

"Dad was more than a little suspicious and asked, 'What else did he say?'"

"He said, 'Tell your dad that when he was a little boy he broke one of the garage windows. He didn't think that I knew, but I did.'"

'No one knew about that window. What did the man look like?'

He was very old with white hair and a cane that had a wolf's head."

My dad stopped the car and looked at me in shock and said, 'That's impossible, that... was grandpa!'"

My father asked me many questions about the man in the garden. I saw grandpa several times again until one day he didn't come anymore. I guess it was at a point in my life when I didn't need him anymore."

38

CHRISTMAS WITH TINA

Mike talked with a local female factory worker named Janie who told Mike that she had breast cancer and would need to have an operation, then radiation, and chemotherapy. She said that she wasn't a driver, but worked at a local factory and lived in the area. So, he asked if there was anything he could do. She told him there was nothing right now, but to pray for her.

She didn't know how she was going to keep everything going with being off from work for all of the treatments. He asked if she was married. She said, "His name is Peter, and we have been divorced for five years."

"Does your ex-husband live in the area?"

"Yes! He is not remarried, but he lives a block from my house."

"Does he know about your cancer?"

"No, I haven't told him."

"Is your relationship so bad that you can't talk with him?"

"No, I guess I should tell him."

"I really think that is best and he might even be able to help you a little."

The next time at the truck stop, Janie told Mike with a big smile on her face, "I did as you suggested, and Peter is going to help me."

They had talked about her cancer treatments and decided that since he was only renting, he would move back in with her (in the spare bedroom) and use the money he was spending on rent to help pay her bills. The problem was they were still short on last month's house payment and Christmas was coming. Janie had a daughter who was not married but had had a child named Tina who was now four years old. Janie was worried that Christmas was still going to be a disaster.

Some of the truckers that knew of the situation, had pitched in with $220, but the house payment was $620. Mike put her name into his church's Hope fundraiser. They gave a check for $400 and some Christmas presents for Tina, her Grandma, and mom. Mike and his friends arranged a party for Tina and her family at Paul's house. Paul was one of the local truckers who helped set it all up. The party was great, and the look on Tina's face was worth the effort.

When Janie opened the envelope and saw the check, she began to cry. Tina asked her grandma, "Grammie, what's the matter?"

"It's okay. Grandma is just very happy."

They continued the celebration with the happiness that warmed their hearts on that cold and snowy

December evening as the presents were opened and appreciated.

Mike heard from Janie or one of her friends often and got an update on her progress. The last that Mike heard was that Peter was still living at Janie's house, and she had had reconstructive surgery and was doing well. She had found a job closer to home, working days for the local community with no more night work. She was now on better terms with Peter than she had ever been. She didn't know if she and Peter would ever get back together, but it was no longer out of the question either.

As far as the question of faith, Janie had told Mike she was starting to get back to church on Sunday mostly because of what Mike and the others had done for her.

Mike felt this was a case of planting the seeds of kindness and waiting for them to grow.

39

THE FIGHTER

Mike met a great looking young man sixteen years of age named Wade and Millie, his mother. Wade was in a wheelchair, and Mike could see that the young man was hurting. He was on his way back from the doctor's office in Chicago, where they were treating him for a degenerative condition that had put him in the wheel chair.

His mother told Mike that all of this had happened in the last two years. But the doctors had stopped the progress of the disease and were hopeful they could start some therapy to help Wade recover some of his motor skills.

The Chaplain didn't seem to make much headway with Wade, but gave him a blessing and said good luck and good-bye.

A couple of weeks later, Wade was there again with his mother. She took Mike aside and said that her son was excited at the prospect of seeing Mike again. It had boosted his spirits, last time, so much and he was looking forward to talking with the Chaplain.

She said that they have had a rough time. She had to quit work to take care of Wade, and with all of the medical expenses, she was at her wit's end and about to give up. The hospital and the state came up with some grants to help with the expenses, but it wasn't enough. She had applied for another grant that would make up the payments and was hopeful she would get it.

Mike went to talk with Wade. He was truly excited, and he told Mike that he was sorry that he was so out of it last time they met. They talked for at least an hour about how hard it has been for him as a teenage boy to get *punched out* with this disease. He had been on the basketball and the track teams, but now he was in a wheelchair. He then said something that stuck Mike as a unique point of view, "It has been a huge adjustment for me and maybe even tougher for my mom. But I am making progress, and I'm thankful for being alive."

Mike was amazed at the wisdom of such a young man.

They also talked about faith and he told Mike, "I have felt the power of the Lord, especially when I have needed Him most."

"Have you told your mom about that?"

"No, I haven't."

"I think you should. She would appreciate hearing about your faith and your positive attitude about healing."

Wade agreed to talk to his mom. He thanked Mike for being there for him and his mom. He apologized again for being a frump when we met two weeks ago.

Mike gave him a blessing and said a prayer for him. Then Wade gave Mike a lasting hug.

Mike saw Wade several more times at widely spaced intervals, then lost track of him and saw him no more. Wade's mom had gotten the additional grant money, and they were doing better financially.

Mike told his wife, "I will never forget the young man's fighting spirit and how he held his head up high through it all. He is a true hero to me. In the midst of all of his own pain and suffering he was worried about his mom."

40

THE REGULAR GUY

Jason was a regular at the truck stop and was a single twenty-nine-year-old factory worker. By the way Jason looked, Mike thought he was a driver and, therefore, didn't even ask. Jason told him much later that he worked in a local factory.

Jason talked about his family (mom, dad, and sisters) and what they would be doing for thanksgiving. He was not super religious, but a God fearing man all the same, and attended a small church most Sundays. He was a very kind man who would do almost anything you asked of him. He was the type that would give the shirt off his back if it was needed.

Mike had many conversations with Jason, because he was there almost every time Mike was there over a period of two years. They talked about sports, the weather, and many other subjects, including faith.

After about two years or so, Jason stopped coming to the truck stop on Mike's night. It made him really concerned, and he asked the restaurant staff if they had seen Jason. No one had seen him for almost three weeks. Mike looked his number up and called his home. His sister answered, and Mike introduced himself.

She said, "Jason is very sick. He has a brain tumor and is in the hospital."

Mike remembered that Jason had said some strange things lately that didn't make sense and was wondering if that was because of the brain tumor.

She said, "Jason had fallen in his apartment and was there for three days unable to get to the phone. I went there with the landlord to check on him and found him on the floor huddled in a corner."

Mike got the name of the hospital and took off work the next day to go to see his friend.

Jason's sister told Mike in the hallway, "The doctors said they can not operate on Jason, because the tumor is so large. Jason knows his condition is terminal and he won't last long."

Jason cheerfully greeted and thanked the Chaplain for taking the time to come see him and asked Mike to pray for him. They said a prayer together and Mike gave him the Lord's blessing.

Mike held his hand in silence for several minutes; it seemed there was nothing more to say.

Mike was certain he would never see his friend again, because his sister was moving him about a hundred miles away to a nursing facility.

About a week later, Mike got a call from Jason's sister, from her home. She said, "They operated on Jason to relieve the pressure in his skull, but there is still no hope."

She asked if Mike would like to come down to see Jason. She knew it was a long way to travel, but Jason had asked. Mike said that he would come down on Friday.

At the truck stop, word got around that that Jason wanted the Chaplain to come down. Ralph, another regular, said that he would like to see Jason as well. So, on Friday they got into Mike's car and went to see Jason. The trip took over three hours to get to the institution.

When they walked in, Jason was subdued but extremely happy to see the two of them. The small group talked for over two hours, until the nurses politely threw them out. They all said their good-byes, and Mike said a prayer for Jason and gave him a blessing.

He told him, "No matter what happens, the Lord will be at your side the whole way."

Jason thanked the Chaplain and Jim for coming then held the Chaplain's hand for a while again, with tears in his eyes. He said he was at peace with the whole thing, especially with the Chaplain coming to be with him.

That was the last time Mike saw Jason alive. He got a call two days later that Jason had died. Several of his friends from the truck stop went to Jason's funeral to wish him peace and say a prayer for him. Jason's sister came over to Mike, gave him a big hug, and thanked him for being there for Jason when he needed him most.

41

MANY STORIES

Chaplain Mike was a witness to many other stories like the following.

Charles from Quebec talked for a long time about his faith and how he found it easier to know God while he was traveling, especially when he was in western Canada looking at all God has made; not what man has changed.

On some nights the conversations were so busy and intense that Mike couldn't remember them later to write them down, and other times they were so profound and filled with the Spirit that he knew this was where he belonged.

A woman driver (an older lady) didn't want to talk at first then told Mike all about how she now drove alone after her husband died a year ago, and how hard it was in this business to be a woman driver who owned her own truck.

They had been team drivers for fourteen years until he died. That actually prepared her for the problems she would face as a driver, owner-operator. She decided to drive alone, partly to help her with her grieving process. But, after getting through the negative attitude from most of the other drivers, dispatchers, and customers, she decided to keep driving.

She didn't like to use the CB radio to talk to other drivers because of all the flak she got as a woman. She was now doing quite well, and she got to travel to where each of her children lives every couple of months. That's a lot better than if she had to pay for travel to go see them.

Mike found out that she was much happier now that she could continue on as a driver. She thanked him and asked for a blessing.

42

GROUP DISCUSSION

On a particularly hot summer afternoon, Mike had a conversation with an "old-timer". Terance was seventy-five years old and had been diving for forty-eight years while he accumulated 4 million miles. The conversation at the restaurant counter soon turned into an open group discussion with three other drivers joining in—Daryl from Milwaukee, David from Des Moines, Ralph from Connecticut, and a young couple in their twenties.

Terance talked about his experiences with the many stories he had to tell, adding how somehow God had a hand in helping him. He also talked about many funny stories and had the whole place laughing. Then the young couple joined the conversation, starting with the wife. She got interested when Daryl told them how God had helped him in several cases.

The wife said, "A month ago we got a bill for three hundred dollars, but didn't have the money. That night we said a prayer for some help. By the end of the week, quite unexpectedly, almost the exact amount of money showed up."

Then, her husband started to talk and join in, "Wow, we couldn't believe it! We knew that the Lord had heard our prayer."

"Then, last week, we were listening to a Christian radio station. It was a great day, and we were enjoying the warm sunshine. I didn't see the four-wheeler come from behind me and swerve in front of my truck. I was just able to avoid the accident by hitting the brakes at the last moment. The crazy drivers out there."

This was one of those occasions when the conversations were so fast and happening at the same time that Mike could not remember all the details later. All he could remember was that it was good for all that participated.

Mike remembered that group discussions or group prayer with the Chaplain were rare. Sometimes, with a little guidance, however, these conversations would be extremely rewarding.

David asked, "Chaplain, could you say a prayer for all of us?"

Mike gave them a blessing and said a short prayer.

They all said thank you to the Chaplain.

43

THE VOICE IN THE ORCHARD

One night after his visit to the truck stop, Mike was talking about families and told his wife Mandy a story about himself. "Years ago, when I was a young boy of ten, my three bothers and I lived on a small farm with Mom and Dad.

"The closest house was about a quarter of a mile away. Our farm had a little of everything from horses, milk cows, pigs, chickens, and... well, you get the idea. We had only fifteen acres, but it was well used to raise the crops we needed for the animals.

"I remember many times when we all pitched in to help hand-pick a corn crop. Other family members like aunts and uncles were invited to help in the harvest, and my mom would cook a meal for all of us to make it into a party. People just don't do that anymore.

"Large trees surrounded the house and barns. The house was set more than a hundred feet back from the road. On the other side of the road were a couple of huge cottonwood trees. Summer breezes would make the leaves of these trees produce the most wonderful rustling sounds of peacefulness. The fields, of course, surrounded the house on both sides. And, on the other side was an apple orchard, which had a summer cottage and a small lake. The cottage was about a quarter of a mile away. The configuration of the land with a swamp and the apple trees made it impossible to hear anyone that was at the cottage.

"The owner of the orchard used the lake for a water supply to irrigate the orchard, but he decided to stock the lake with largemouth bass. We boys thought this was a great idea, especially since we knew the owner, and he allowed us to use the lake any time we wanted, for swimming and fishing.

"At our house we had a large back porch, where we often ate our summer meals. It was so peaceful and quiet in the country. Even when the orchard owner had a party at the cottage, we hardly ever heard them at our porch.

"My father was a handy man and was always working on some project around the farm. We boys always liked to play outside and spent many hours in the yard.

"One day we were all outside. Father was working, cutting some boards for the trim on the porch. He was making quite some racket with the table saw and then hammering nails into the trim pieces in place.

"One of my brothers and I went to the porch to ask Mom for some cold water. My other two brothers were out in the yard. Dad was still making noise with his project. All of a sudden, Dad said, 'Did you hear that?'

Everyone looked at him, and Mom said, 'How could you hear anything, with all the noise you are making?'

"We all stopped to listen, but all we heard was the rustle of leaves in the trees from the gentle summer breeze. Mom said, 'You must have imagined it.' We all went back to what we were doing.

"About a half-hour later, Dad heard the voice again and asked us to all be quiet. He asked if we heard it. Mom asked, 'Heard what?' He said, 'It sounded like a woman crying for help.' We all listened intently, but there was no voice. We brothers spread out all around the yard, to see if we could hear anything. Again, we heard and saw nothing.

"Soon, we were all back to whatever we were doing. Father was making even more noise because he had a long board to cut. In the middle of sawing the board, he heard the voice again and shouted for everyone to be quiet. But we heard nothing. This time, Father said that he heard a woman tell him she needed help. Mom asked, 'How could you have heard anything with all of the sawing noise?' 'I don't know, but I did hear it,' he said.

"Dad decided to walk over to the cottage to see if there was anyone there. I went with him. When we arrived, we found a woman, who had fallen on the dock. She had gone out early in the morning to fish. She wasn't watching, tripped on a rope, broke her leg, and landed in the water's edge. The rope got tangled around her ankle and prevented her from being able to get out of the water. It was now four o'clock in the afternoon. She was in a lot of pain and already quite weak from being in the water for so long. It was all she could do to talk softly to us.

"Dad asked her if she had been calling for someone to help her. She said she had given up on that idea this morning. She was too weak to holler, but she had just been praying that God would help her stay afloat and send someone to help her.

"We helped her out of the water, and I ran home to ask Mom to call an ambulance for the woman.

"The really important part of this story is; how had Dad heard the woman. She was too weak to shout so how could Dad hear her. He was also close to the noise the saw was making and had heard her. He was the only one who heard her."

Mandy asked, "What do you think, Mike?"

"I think the Lord does hear us, when we need him most. All we need to do is ask."

Even Jesus said, "Father I know that you hear me. You always hear me. "

"Keep on asking, and you will be given what you ask for. Keep on looking, and you will find. Keep on knocking, and the door will be opened. For everyone who asks, receives. Everyone who seeks, finds. And the door is opened to everyone who knocks" (Matt 7: 7-8).

44

A YOUNG FRIEND

F rancois was in his fifties and had a weekly route from Idaho to Chicago and back. He was a very pleasant person with graying hair, a very small beard, and a slight French accent. Francois was currently dating a woman who was only thirty-five years old. I say dating, but it was more of a close friendship in which he was helping her with her bills and seeing her once a month or so. Francois was very happy for the friendship, but he was very cautious at any thought of this becoming anything serious.

The woman had been divorced for two years and was really struggling to support her three daughters. Francois said he met her at an event at the Catholic Church, where he played the organ on Sundays.

She lived in a town one hour from his house, which was one of the reasons that they only got together once a month. The other reason was his travel schedule.

Francois really liked the woman, but he was afraid that the age difference was too much of an obstacle. He and Mike talked for about an hour, then he said he had to go to sleep, as he had to get up at 3:00 a.m. Mike gave him a blessing, and they parted.

Mike saw Francois again several times, then several months later, he told Mike that he and his woman friend were going to Florida for vacation. Mike asked him if he thought it was a good idea. He said, "We talked about the age difference and decided that we will see where it goes, because she has no real problem with it and she likes being with me."

When Francois got back, he came into the truck stop and told Mike all about the wonderful time they had on holidays in Florida.

He showed Mike some pictures of them at the beach.

Mike said, "Wow, she sure is good looking."

"Yeah, she is a real looker," Francois proudly said.

A month later, Francois announced they were getting married and he was going to sell his place and move to her house.

Mike asked, "So, everything is fine and working out?"

"Yes, except for two of her daughters, who don't trust me and won't talk to me."

"Francois, my friend, are you sure this is going to work?"

"Yes, I have thought about it for some time and the two of us have discussed it at length. I think it will be fine."

"What about your organ playing at church?"

"I will have to find a new church in her town, and I will still play at my church once a month."

He was convinced, and Mike could see that Francois was extremely happy, but he secretly worried for him.

He told Francois, "I'll pray for you."

So, Mike said a prayer for them on his way home.

Mike saw Francois many times over the next year and found out that the relationship was falling apart. They eventually separated and got a divorce. Francois was told that she had found someone younger who lived and worked in her town. He was extremely saddened but said that he understood. He said, "I am much older than she is, and I am gone most of the time. I suppose I knew this was inevitable, but I was blinded by love. I would not have given up the chance to be loved by her for anything, and I am still happy for it.

"It seems ironic. I was finally getting along fine with all three daughters."

45

HOMELESS

There was a homeless person at the truck stop that didn't need any help or a meal or anything, but he wanted to talk to the Chaplain. Evan was dressed in clean clothes, but his body looked the part of a homeless person. Although he was clean-shaven and his hair was cut, he was very thin and looked malnourished. Mike convinced Evan to let the Chaplain provide a meal. Evan was very grateful.

Over the years, Mike had heard many stories from homeless people. Some of these stories were hard to believe. They seemed like a stretch of the imagination, beyond reasonable doubt. Evan's story was very much like that.

It was late fall and winter was coming, but Evan lived in his car at the truck stop. It was still warm enough out, so it was okay.

Evan told Mike that he owned a company and was on his way to Kentucky to buy a ranch, where he could bring his four horses, which were being boarded at a local farm. The boarding fees were expensive, but he had no alternative. He was living at the truck stop, because he was waiting for a court settlement on the sale of his company.

He said, "When it comes through, I'll have my four horses hauled down to Kentucky and get all set up on the new ranch. There is a small barn there now, so I'll have to build a house, but I need the money to make it all happen."

He told Mike that he had some living money and showed him a wad of cash. He said that he needed to conserve his cash, because he didn't know how long the settlement might take.

Evan was at the truck stop till March of the following year, and Mike talked to him many times. The truck stop manager had been very kind to Evan and allowed him to hang around inside of the restaurant, but that was wearing thin.

After Evan left on his trip, Mike found out that it was all true. He did have four horses that someone was boarding for him for a fee. He left when he got his settlement, hired a truck to haul the horses and went to Kentucky.

It just goes to show you that you may not believe all that you hear at the truck stop, but sometimes even the wildly fantastic can be all true (or at least mostly true).

46

THE DRIVING GAME

Mike sat with a couple who were not drivers. They introduced themselves as Francine and William. The conversation, lasting for quite some time, centered on their family and their children.

Francine finally asked, "What makes driving truck so hard?"

Mike explained, "The government (DOT or Department of Transportation) has a law that states that a truck driver can only drive eleven hours a day. In addition, many companies have put a speed control on their trucks, set to a maximum of 65 miles per hour. In effect, the government controls the maximum you can make, but not the minimum you can make. This is no game.

Other parts of the law specify that you must take a ten-hour rest period at the end of eleven hours of driving time or total of fourteen hours of on-duty time."

Mike gave them an example, "For instance, you start your day at 3:30 a.m., have a bite to eat and at 4 a.m., and head to the local terminal to get a load. It's only ten miles, and they load you right away. Great! That only took you thirty minutes. The next drop and load is in the city and is listed as 98 miles. This should be good, drive 98 miles on the expressway to the city to drop one and pick up another load. And at 4:30 a.m. this should be a piece of cake. However, there has been an accident and you are soon stopped in traffic, which takes you three and half hours (instead of just under two hours). You look at your odometer and see that you have already traveled 120 miles today. You finally get to the dock, but because you are late you get put at the end of the queue and wait for an hour to get loaded and on your way for an eight-mile partial pickup.

Let's assume you traveled a whopping 368 miles got paid for 298 miles and spent twelve hours. Almost 300 miles at 30 cents per mile is $89.40 for twelve and a half hours work or $7.15 per hour. A week at that rate would only be $630 before tax.

But don't worry; there will be better days (and there will be worse days). Maybe you can see the frustration in being a truck driver."

Francine and William thanked Mike for the example and said good-bye.

47

MY PLAN

On some occasions Mike was tired (aka lazy) and didn't feel very much like traveling over thirty miles in traffic to get to the truck stop. Somehow, he found the fortitude to get off his bottom and get on the road. As you may know, our Lord has a sense of humor. We may think we have a plan, but it may not be the plan the Lord has in mind for us, so guess who wins?

On several occasions as Mike was contemplating leaving early, or not going to the truck stop at all, he would get surprised. On one such occasion, he made the feeble attempt to say, "It looks like snow. I'd better not go."

Mandy, his wife of forty years knew him quite well and said, "I just looked at the weather channel, and they said that it is only flurries."

Mike easily relented as he looked outside and swiftly said, "Hey, it looks like it is not accumulating. I guess I should go."

He thought he was being clever by making it his own idea.

On that occasion, when he arrived at the truck stop and walked into the restaurant, one of the waitresses came up to him at the door and said, "There's a driver in the second booth that has been waiting for you."

Mike thanked her and went to the man's booth, thinking, *Wow! That's never happened before.*

Mike introduced himself and the man said, "Please sit down, Chaplain."

He said he was having a problem with his wife, and he explained the situation to Mike, as the man began to see the solution on his own.

While they were talking, a man from the hallway peered over the edge of the booth to say, "I'd like to talk to you, Chaplain, when you are through."

Then, within thirty seconds, another man sitting at a table on the other side of their booth, said, "I need to talk to you also, padre."

Needless to say, Mike realized that the Lord had a plan that night, (which was not the one Mike had loosely concocted for himself). The Lord didn't just have one person who needed a chaplain, but three at the same time. Mike got the message in a dramatic way. He didn't have much resistance to going to the truck stop from then on.

48

THE JOURNALIST

On another occasion, Mike got to the truck stop, and the head waitress came to him, winked and said, "There is a pretty young lady in the booth over there that wants to talk to you."

The lady was a journalism student and had gotten permission from the General Manager to interview drivers about trucking. She said to Mike, "I found out from the truckers that they like to come to this truck stop because there is a chaplain here and it is safe. They think that there are no lot-lizards (it's the trucker term for lady-of-the-night) here because there is a chaplain. What is a chaplain?"

She was very interested in finding out what a truck stop chaplain did. Mike explained the ministry of presence and how he helped travelers to feel at home.

She was amazed that a minister would come all the way out to the truck stop and take time with the drivers. She later told the truck stop manager that Mike was the reason that many drivers like to stop here and management should support the Chaplain. He agreed with her.

He later told Mike, "I have also been told by drivers that they liked to talk to the chaplain here. He doesn't push and get in our face. He gives us a place to talk about our family, our faith and our needs and concerns. Please keep him around."

49

400 POUND DRIVER

B en had been at the truck stop many times, but never took the time to really talk to the Chaplain. Ben was very rough, loud, harsh, and extremely overweight. Mike had had brief conversations with him, but never anything in-depth. Then, one night Ben sat and told Mike that he hauled cattle feed and other bulk items for his company.

In talking with the man, Mike discovered that he was actually quite nice and very interesting.

Ben continued, "I am now on a diet, and the doctor has me on 1200 calories a day."

"Wow! How are you doing with the diet?"

He said, "It's really very tough, especially eating at truck stops. But I've lost forty pounds in a month."

"That's great! I'm sure you will feel better when you shed some of those pounds. How heavy were you when you started the diet?"

"I was four hundred pounds when I first went to the doctor's office. But this is not really a diet, it's a life style change. I have had to completely change what and how I eat."

Ben talked about his eating habits he had changed and how the doctor wanted him to eat six to eight small meals a day.

Ben said, "Yeah, like that's going to happen, being a truck driver and all. I only get paid for the miles I drive, not for the time I spend in restaurants."

Mike suggested that he purchase some healthy snack food to eat in the truck, not chips and soda. He thought that was a great idea.

The next week Ben actually looked thinner, and he proudly reported that he had lost another ten pounds for a total of fifty pounds. They talked more about his diet and how that was affecting his life.

Ben told Mike all of this had happened after his divorce. Mike asked some questions about that and Ben went into some detail.

He said, "Yeah, my wife left me after I lost the business and started driving to feed the family."

"You had a business?"

"Sure did. It was a family owned business that we were grooming and growing into a public corporation."

"What kind of business was it?"

"We had a production company for video, audio, and computer training programs."

"So, what happened?"

"My family consisted of me, two brothers, and Dad who ran the production company. Then in the 80s, the bottom dropped out of the training market, and Dad died. We were still doing great, and profits were even up. Then the bank got nervous and told us we had to refinance our loan, but they would not offer us a loan. Well, that was not a good time to go looking for a $700,000 loan on video production equipment and a small building.

"We ended up having to sell everything to pay the bank. Sure, the three brothers ended up with enough cash for each of us to buy homes for cash, but our family business and our livelihood was gone!

"I had just gotten married and needed to find a job with enough income to pay the bills and take care of my new wife. I decided to start truck driving, and as I got better at it, I made more money. The problem was that I was gone all the time.

"This went on for fifteen years or more, and my wife told me that she was unhappy being alone all the time.

"She told me, she didn't get married to spend her life alone.

"But I was too busy making more money. She finally got my attention when she said she would leave me if I don't get a job closer to home and be home at night. So, I changed jobs to be a local driver, but I guess it was too late to make a difference by that time.

"I don't blame her entirely, but here I was in this mess. I just gave up, and I just didn't care anymore. My life was a total mess. My dad died, the family business that I really enjoyed was lost, and my wife left me. So, I put myself totally into driving the truck and food was my only comfort. After all, it was not harmful, so I ate. Now, don't kid yourself I was never a small person.

Even as a high school sophomore I was a two hundred and thirty-pound football player.

"I didn't actually realize how big I was getting until one day I told myself that I was tired of looking like this, and I made an appointment with a doctor. Now, I am committed to change. I don't know how much I can lose, but I am not dieting—I have changed my entire life as well as what and how much I eat."

Mike told Ben that he would pray that he would be able to stick with it and get his weight down. He thanked Mike for spending time with him and said, "I hope your house sale goes through."

Mike could have pushed Ben more about his faith, but felt he needed to get some results with his non-diet first.

50

RALPH FROM OHIO

Ralph was sitting at the counter, two seats from Mike. He looked relatively happy as he made some friendly comments to the waitress, so Mike said hi and told him he was the chaplain. Ralph seemed to brighten with that revelation.

He told Mike that he had been married for a year and a half and had a child, who was now six months old. They talked about some other general information, and he told Mike he was an evangelical. Mike immediately thought, *Oh boy, here we go.*

Ralph was very open to talking about what he felt about faith but also willing to listen to Mike's feelings. He even asked if Mike was affiliated with the Truck Stop Ministries, Inc. He told Ralph that he was not and his ministry was different. He asked what church Mike was affiliated with. He told him a Catholic church about thirty miles away. Ralph's eyes widened and said that he was amazed that a catholic was out here at a truck stop.

He was very happy that Mike had decided to minister at the truck stop; it was very much needed and appreciated. They talked about that for a while then about the healthcare reform and other social issues. Since the restaurant was not busy and there were only two other tables occupied, they continued their friendly chat for another hour.

When Ralph got up to go he said God Bless you and Mike said the same to him. Mike also said, "God bless your family and keep you safe on the roads."

Mike felt he could have spent more time on the faith issue, but Ralph seemed to be at peace with the faith they shared and Ralph was the one that changed the subject and said he had to get his rig moving.

51

THE MAN FROM EGYPT

Ahmed worked as a busboy in the restaurant. Mike had said hello to him a couple of times, and he returned the greeting. The man always seemed to be a hard worker and always tackling some task around the restaurant. Mike could see from the way the man looked that he was from the Middle East, but they hadn't had the time to talk.

One night Ahmed wasn't too busy and stopped by to say hello, then he started to talk to Mike.

He said, "My name Ahmed. I am Christian. I am Christian."

Mike instantly realized there was a huge language barrier as he said, "That's great! My name is Mike. Where are you from?"

"I no speak English much. I from Egypt."

Mike found speaking with Ahmed very difficult. He could see the man was struggling to find the words and what he did say often did not make sense. Mike did find out that Ahmed was married and had one child.

Ahmed then said that he must get back to work, and Mike gave him a blessing.

Mike continued on with his ministering to the truckers and when he was finished for the night, he exited the truck stop. As he got into his car and started the engine, Ahmed came to the car window and tapped on it to get Mike's attention. Now, you have to remember this was only six months after the attacks of 9/11, and we were all very jittery anyway. So, at first it frightened Mike, and he was looking the other way when the tapping began. Then Mike turned and saw Ahmed very close to his car window. He jumped, quickly calmed down and rolled down the window as Ahmed said in very clear English, "Please help me!"

Mike turned off the engine, and the man told him in not so clear English,

"I need...drive..."

He made a face as he tried to find the words. He then drew a square with his index fingers. Mike must have looked very puzzled, because Ahmed reached out and gently touched Mike's arm. He tried again and said, "Driver test."

Mike said, "You need to take the driver's test?"

He said, "Yes!" with a great sigh of relief.

As he talked and Mike interpreted, it was determined that he had taken the driver's test more than once, but failed. His wife had to take him to work and come get him at the end of his shift, each day. He really needed to pass the test. Then he placed his hands on Mike's arm at the window and looked at him pleadingly as he asked, "Please help!"

Mike determined that the man's language barrier was a real problem at the DMV testing facility. He had passed the written test, but in the driving test it was difficult to understand the things the testing officer was saying to Ahmed. The result for the last two attempts was failure and frustration. Mike made a date for Wednesday morning to take Ahmed to the testing station and see what could be done.

Mike later told his wife, "I am at a loss. After all what can I do? I can't be in the car with him when he is taking the test. I am also afraid of inviting a stranger into my car."

It's one of those things drilled into your head, "Never let a stranger into your car." What if they pull a gun or want to harm you—you're trapped. But, Mike decided to see if he could help his newfound Christian friend.

On the appointed morning Mike decided to wear his Truck Stop Chaplain shirt. After all he was doing a Chaplain's activity and it couldn't have hurt to have that recognized. He also took off work and traveled the thirty miles to the truck stop to pick up Ahmed.

Michael drove Ahmed's car as he gave directions to the testing facility, which was twenty-five miles further away. He told Mike about his family who came with him to America to have a better life. So far it hadn't turned out that way. He told the Chaplain it is very difficult to get any kind of job, if you don't know English very well. He said if he were Hispanic, there would be all kinds of help for him to understand the language, but not for him in his language. He was trying to learn English with the help of his wife, who spoke it much better than he did.

When they arrived at the testing facility and he signed-in, Mike got really worried that he would not be of any help. When Ahmed's name was called, Mike walked out with him and the testing officer. Mike introduced himself and said, "I came with Ahmed today to ask that you have some patience with my friend who doesn't speak English very well."

The officer looked at Mike's Truck Stop Chaplain shirt and said that he could not go with Ahmed, but it would be okay.

They got into Ahmed's car, and the officer took his time explaining to the man. When they got back, the officer looked at Mike and said, "He did fine!"

As they drove back to the truck stop, Ahmed told Mike he was very happy and said he was out of words. At the truck stop, he thanked Mike, and his wife came running out to find out how the test had gone. Ahmed told her in his language what had happened and she was extremely happy and gave the Chaplain a big hug.

She told Mike as she hugged her husband, "This will be a big help because I have had to wake up our school aged child to come get Ahmed from work in the middle of the night. Now he will be able to drive himself. God bless you!"

In the following weeks, Ahmed told Mike more, and the Chaplain could see he was learning more English, which made it easier to communicate with him. Mike learned that he was working two jobs and his wife worked also to get enough money for his family to survive. He wanted to get a better job but needed to learn more English. It was difficult because there were no places locally for ESL (English as a Second Language) classes in his native language.

One evening Ahmed came to Mike and asked, "Please help me!" Mike asked him what he needed help with. He said he needed to get a computer.

Mike had seen a special in the paper and told Ahmed, "Go to Best Buy with your wife and talk to them."

The next week Ahmed came to Mike again and said, "I can't get the computer because I have no credit."

Mike asked, "Do you have a bank where you keep your money."

"Yes, I do."

"See if the bank could work out a credit plan."

The next week he was very happy and told Mike that he had gone to the bank, got a loan and got the computer on sale. Ahmed was very happy and was now learning English much faster.

It seemed to Mike that it was amazing the results that come from simple efforts.

52

THE MARKETING EXECUTIVE

As Mike sat at the counter, he noticed a man across the way. He looked like Mr. Clean from television a few years ago, but more like a wrestler with a shaved head and a lean muscular build. Not someone you would want to get into a heated disagreement with. Mike noticed that he was drawing something and asked him, "What are you drawing, if you don't mind me asking?"

"It is a design for a multilevel house built into a hillside," the man replied.

Then he proceeded to tell more from across the double counters. Mike was having difficulty hearing, so he went around to the man's side who motioned for Mike to be seated.

After he explained about the house, he told Mike he was from North Carolina and was on his way home. Then he said, "Actually, I have no home, except that metal box outside.

"By the way, my name is Dave."

"I'm Mike. Do you have family back in North Carolina, Dave?"

"No. But…where do I start? Well, a few years ago, in 1985, I owned my own successful graphics design company. We built very sophisticated slide shows for our high-end customers. Before that I worked for a man named Dick who built and owned the company. He ran the business out of his beautiful two-story home with the first floor as the office and the second floor was his residence. All was going quite well until Dick's drinking caused him to start having Alzheimer's like symptoms. I asked him a couple of times to let me purchase the business from him, but he always said no. It all came to a head one day when a big customer called me to ask how his $50,000 graphics job was coming along. As it was due in three days, he wanted to know if he could see some of the layouts.

"I was shocked, but kept it professional and said with confidence, 'Let me check on it and call you right back.' I hung up the phone and went to Dick's office to find out where this important customer's job was. Dick told me, 'I have no idea. I didn't know we had a job from them.' I looked around Dick's office with him and found the folder under his pencil sharpener. Dick couldn't even remember getting the job from the client. The team and I worked far into the night to have something to present to the client the next day.

"I am not a praying man, but on the way back to the office after the presentation, I said a prayer, 'Please God, help me to find a way to take over the company and hopefully save it from Dick.' I was really feeling the pressure of trying to save this job and keep the company going without any idea of how I could make it happen. All of a sudden, I got very emotional and had to pull over to collect myself.

"I pulled over to the side of the expressway. It took a few minutes until I felt I was gaining some control over the anger, the lack of sleep, and all of the emotions. Then, I looked up ahead and saw a huge picture of Christ on a billboard. The caption said, 'Now is the time.' Well, I really lost it. I got this feeling of a presence, and at the same time, my skin turned to goose bumps. I felt frightened, but at peace at the same time. At the very moment that I needed inspiration; there it was. Was this a sign that I would be able to take over the business? I didn't know all the answers, but I felt the Holy Spirit was with me.

"I took a few more minutes to settle down and got back on the road to the office. It was after six p.m. when I got to the office, and from the driveway I could see Dick sitting in the receptionist's chair waiting for me. I didn't know what he had in mind, but I went in to face the music, as they say. When I walked in Dick just said in a low tone, 'So, you still want to buy the business?'"

"I was blown away and said, 'Sure if I can afford it.'"

"We worked out the deal for $75,000 for the business, all the equipment, and the great old house. An incredible deal, I'll have to admit.

"I still to this day wonder how God eased my fears on the expressway. Was the fact that I stopped right at the spot where I could see the picture of Jesus, a sign meant for me? Could God have also changed Dick's mind to make me that incredible offer?"

Mike told Dave, "I believe God does give us signs to help us find the path and to help us to understand that He is always with us."

Dave agreed and continued with his story.

"I ran the business for several years, and we used some state of the art computers for the time. Today's computers are so much faster that there would be no comparison. We were doing very well working with the big-boys, until Intel announced the Pentium computer, which allowed my customers to do what we did as a specialty.

"So, I lost my business. My wife left me and my daughter..."

Dave started to get emotional.

"I loved her so much...she died."

Dave stopped talking and started to wipe his eyes. Mike reached out and touched his hand and said, "It's okay to have feelings of loss even after a long time."

It took several minutes before Dave was able to say anything. The story and the feelings expressed were so strong that Mike had to wipe his eyes as he tried to fight back his own tears and his trembling lower lip. Then Dave barely squeaked out, "She was a good girl, and I still miss her terribly."

Dave was silent again for a few more minutes as both men shared a few more tears. Then he continued, "She was killed in an automobile accident. So, after all of that, I decided to become a truck driver."

They were silent again.

Mike tried to lighten it up.

"How is it going with driving a truck? Are you making any money?"

"No! Two weeks ago, I got a check for three hundred dollars, and the next week it was a hundred and sixty, and last week it was seven hundred fifty dollars."

"How can you possibly survive on so little income?"

"I can't. I just hope it gets better. I can't wait to see this week's check."

Mike talked with Dave for two and a half hours. Mike told him about a class that he had taken on humor in the gospels and started to tell him one of the stories.

Dave stopped Mike and said, "You need to talk to my sister about scripture. I am not the one."

"Let me tell you just one short story."

After the first story, Dave encouraged Mike to tell several more. Afterward, he said he really enjoyed hearing those stories.

One of the stories Mike told him was, "In the Gospel of Matthew, there is a passage that says, 'If a soldier demands that you carry his gear for a mile, carry it two miles.'

"Well, in their culture at that time of Roman occupation, soldiers were allowed to command the Jews to carry the army's materials for not more than a mile or the soldier would be in trouble with his superior officer. So, if you said you would go two miles was that a form of peaceful protest?"

Mike said, "I don't know for sure what was meant, but all I am saying is that the Gospels were meant to be stories that make us think from our heart not just to read the words and say, 'That's what it means!'

"In second Corinthians, we are told, 'it is carved not in stone, but on human hearts.'"

Dave then said, "You have really done your job, Chaplain. You have gotten me to talk about all kinds of personal issues that I have not been able to discuss with anyone. You have brought out emotions that I have had hidden, and you have brought faith to me that I thought was lost. We have shared laughter, tears for my departed daughter, joy, memories, and the Spirit of God. God Bless you. "

Mike asked if he could say a prayer with Dave who said yes as he reached across the table for Mike's hands. The Chaplain said a short prayer and gave Dave a blessing and told him that he would pray that God would show Dave a path to some work he can really enjoy. He thanked Mike again and said good-bye.

53

LAUGHABLE

Not all of the stories from the truck stop were so serious. Some were gut-splitting comedies. Donna told a story about the time she was in a restaurant, sitting at the counter, when an old man came to sit next to her. In talking to him, she found out that he was eighty-seven years old and was hard of hearing. She was only thirty-five, so the older man was ancient to her. Donna worked in the city and lived out near the truck stop.

She had a great time talking with the old man and heard all about his family. He told her he was deaf in his other ear and hard of hearing in the ear closest to her. He was, therefore, able to hear her few remarks and questions, because she was right next to him.

When they were done, the old man got up to go and started walking away. She looked in his direction and saw a stream of white material hanging out of the man's pant leg. She thought to herself that it must be toilet paper. She tried to call out to him but he could not hear her and kept walking away. She didn't want him to be embarrassed, so she ran up behind him and decided to step on the toilet paper to rid the man of any problem with it.

As she stepped on the paper, the man instantly fell forward. Luckily he caught himself against a pillar and avoided a dangerous fall on the floor.

She was terribly embarrassed and explained to him what she was trying to do and he laughed, as he said, "That wasn't toilet paper—it was an elastic ankle bandage."

They both had a good laugh, and she apologized.

54

HELD PRISONER

Mike met TR, who was a homeless person at the truck stop. He was a rather clean homeless person about fifty years old, who said he did not need anything, except to talk. He told Mike that his name was T.R. and that he had been able to hitch rides from town to town without much trouble except right after 9/11, when it became really tough to trust anyone enough to let a rider into your vehicle. He wanted to wait till tomorrow to go out to the corner and attempt to get a ride.

TR liked to be at truck stops where he could get some food, take a shower, and talk to other drivers.

He told Mike several things, and then he said, "Years ago I used to work for a circus. You would not believe what that's all about."

"What do you mean?"

"Well, they used to take in all sorts of guys to help with the grunt work. So, in the evening, they would put the grunts in cages for the night."

Michael was aghast, "In cages? What kind of cages?"

"These were big cages like the ones used for wild animal acts during the shows. We had bunks and all the things we needed, but we were locked in at night."

"Wow! That sounds a bit like slavery. Why did they do that?"

"Well, it was actually for our own good, as some of the guys used to go into the towns and cause trouble or just wander off, so they decided to lock us in at night. When we signed on, we had to agree to being locked up each night, for our own safety."

"Was it interesting, setting up the tents in each town?"

"Yeah, it was. But it got boring after a while, doing the same thing each day or every other day. I got out of it after only one season, but some guys were at it for many years. The money wasn't that good, and you were off during the winter. I guess you had to be a carnie to keep doing that."

TR explained that a carnie was a person who worked the carnivals. Mike probed gently and found out that TR had been married with no kids, when his wife suddenly died of cancer. He hated his job, so he quit and sold his home. He had an insurance policy that was paying him a small amount each month.

They talked more, and Mike asked him if there was anything could do for him.

TR told Mike there was nothing he needed, and he lived his life the way he wanted, always traveling to new places with no worries to tie him down. He said, "God takes care of me."

Mike could see that TR was very tired and needed to find real rest. TR's face was drawn and very thin. His hair (what little there was of it) was kind of a dirty gray and shabby. The man's face really showed his age, with dark bags under his dark brown deep-set eyes.

Mike gave TR a blessing and said a prayer for him that he would find peace. As they parted, Mike said another private prayer that TR would find a home to rest his weary bones and have a place to grow old with friends.

That was definitely one of those times when Mike had to say to himself, "I find that story hard to believe, but in this ministry, you never know."

55

IN A FIELD

A man named George was wearing an oil-stained, heavy winter coat even though the temperature outside was only 42 degrees. The man also had a slight limp as he strode over to the counter to take a seat near the Chaplain.

Mike said hello as the man seated himself. He noticed the man had deep-set eyes that caught his attention. They finished the introductions, then George told Mike his story. He said, "I have been driving for twenty years and have seen all kinds of things on the road. A couple of winters ago, I was driving in a snowstorm and thought as I drove, *This is the worst weather I've ever driven in.*"

George lived in South Dakota with his wife of twelve years and three children. Snowy weather was no surprise to him, but this storm came up so fast that he became alarmed.

"It was accumulating so fast, that I couldn't adjust my driving to match what was happening," he said.

He was hauling a light load of filters to Milwaukee from Bettendorf, Iowa. He told Mike, "A light load is worse than a heavy load in a snowstorm, as the heavy load puts more pressure on the tires and the road which gives better traction."

The trip started out just fine for the first hour, then the weather turned ugly in the next ten minutes. He had heard on the radio that it was turning much colder. The roads were now like glass, it was late and there were no other vehicles on the road, so he planned to pull off at the next exit to get out of this mess.

As George got to the exit, he hit a patch of black-ice and his truck lost control, even though he had been going slow. The truck skidded off the road where there was no real ditch, so it kept going toward a steep embankment, sloping away from the roadway. Now, the truck gained speed, sliding down the hill like a sled, until it glanced off a tree on the passenger side and kept going to the bottom of the hill. It finally came to rest in a bunch of smaller trees and shrubs far from the roadway.

George regained consciousness, but he didn't know how long he had been out. He looked at the clock on the dash, but it was smashed and not working. It had stopped at 11:45.

He tried to move his legs, but realized he was caught by some part of the dashboard and couldn't move. It was dark, and all of the truck lights were out, but there was a gentle glow in his cab reflected off the snow. He called it snow light.

He said, "Snow light is a condition where the white snow reflected light off the clouds and brightened the night."

After some minutes his eyes adjusted to be able to see some things. He looked at his watch. It took him a few minutes to make out the dial positions and figured he had been out for thirty minutes. George knew he was in real trouble here. The rate at which the snow was covering his tracks and his vehicle, no one would be able to see that his truck had gone off the road, and he was hidden in the bushes, so they would not be able to find him.

It was getting incredibly cold in the cab, because the windows were all broken and the temperature was falling. The lights were all out on his rig, but he tried to get his foot to the brake pedal. Maybe if he pushed on the brakes he might get the taillights to light up. After working on this for many minutes, he was able to get his foot to the edge of the brake and pushed. Nothing happened.

Now he was really worried. He was injured and could feel blood on his shirt, and it was getting colder by the minute. He was only wearing a light shirt and slacks and that would not protect him from the cold. He guessed it was only 19 or 20 degrees at this point with a twenty mile per hour wind. We're talking wind-chill here.

George decided all he could do was to pray and realized he may be meeting his Maker very soon. He said, "Lord, I know I have not been close to you. I am sorry for that. Please help me deal with this situation. And help my family."

Almost immediately, there was a sparking noise from the front of the truck, and the lights flashed on. George's hopes were filled with joy and thanksgiving. The lights, however, were only on for a few seconds then went off again. He was now really bewildered. What had just happened? If the Lord was helping him, what kind of help was it to have only a couple of seconds of lights?

George awaited the inevitable. He would freeze to death here in the bushes and wouldn't be found for days. He thought, *What a terrible thing for my family. I truly love my wife. She will be destroyed by my death. I can't bear to think of the sadness that will cause her. And the kids, they will miss their dad. But here I am stuck with no hope for being saved.*

As he was drifting in and out of consciousness and thinking of his family, he said more prayers for them. In his half-conscious state, he thought he felt heat. All of a sudden, he heard the sound of the wind that made his skin crawl. Then he heard it again and realized that there was another familiar sound mixed in. He listened again and heard a siren. And he saw the faint red glow of flashing lights in the snow.

Within two minutes there was a policeman at his side with a blanket. He told George he had seen the brake lights flash in the bushes. It took another half-hour to get George out of the truck onto a stretcher.

In the warmth of the ambulance, the policeman asked how long he had been there. George asked what time it was. They told him 2:00 a.m. He said, "That makes it around two and quarter hours."

"How is that possible to be out in that cold for over two hours without heat and with no coat?" the Policeman said.

The EMT added, "It's not possible. You would have frozen to death in a matter of minutes. It's only ten degrees with the wind-chill."

The officer then asked, "I also have to ask if you had a passenger?"

"No, I was alone. Why do you ask?"

"Well, we found an impression in the snow where the snow was melted in the shape of another person sitting next to you in the wreckage of the cab. We did not find the person and were wondering where they went."

"Well, I don't know. All I know is that the heater in the truck must have provided the warmth that I felt and kept me from freezing."

"That's impossible. All power in the truck was off."

After the truck was pulled out of the snow and back to the shop, they discovered the battery was completely smashed and had no chance of supplying any power.

So, how had the brake lights flashed, with no power in the truck?

Who was that in the cab next to George?

How was he able to feel heat when the heater wasn't working?

56

FOOD FOR THOUGHT

Mike met Dennis, who was a friendly man with the bluest eyes Mike had ever seen. Mike was not in the habit of noticing eye color, especially of men. But Dennis's eyes were bright and not deep-set, so they were very noticeable.

Dennis told him about growing up in rural Arkansas in the late fifties. He told Mike, "We lived in a very rural area where in a twenty square mile section of country there were only four to six houses. My parents grew vegetables and did well. We weren't rich, but we weren't hurting either.

"The area we lived in was very peaceful, and there was never any threat of crime. In fact, we never had locks on the doors. Heck, no one ever came down our road unless they had some specific business there. Our house was located near two other houses in such a way that you could just see the driveway to each of the other two houses from the end of our driveway.

"My family had two hundred fifty acres with an irrigation system. So, all you had to do was plant your crops and hit the switches to start the irrigation system then turn it off again at the end of the cycle and harvest the crops.

"My parents gave a lot of food away to help those that needed it. In reality, there was no way to send all the food to market that we could harvest.

"One time we all went to town to shop for clothes for the coming school season. We were gone most of the day, but when we got home, Mom discovered the back door was ajar and someone had entered our house.

"Mom was very calm and asked us all to settle down and look all around the house to see what was missing. The children all took their own bedrooms. She took the kitchen and Dad took the rest of the house.

"After the search was complete, we all reported that nothing was missing and nothing even seemed to have been touched. All the televisions were still in their places. Nothing was missing, not even the stereo. We were all puzzled until it was Mom's turn to report on the kitchen. She told us the pantry door was open and some of the food was gone.

"About that time one of our neighbors had seen us drive up and came over to let Mom and Dad know they had seen two of the new neighbors' boys walking up our driveway.

"Mom gave me two cardboard boxes and asked me and the other children to go fill the boxes with food from storage. I thought we were getting food for our pantry. When we returned, Dad asked us to put the food in the trunk of the car.

"Then our parents packed all three children and themselves into the car and headed down the road to the new neighbor's house. We thought, *Those boys are going to get it now.*

"Once we arrived at the Johnsons', we were told to be polite. Dad and Mom said hello to them and introduced all of us, all neighborly like. They talked about how hard times were and how hard it was to feed a family.

"Mom asked if they had any children. They said, 'Yes, of course, we should have introduced our two boys.'

"Mr. Johnson called through the screen door into the house for the boys to come out. They were introduced, then Dad asked Mr. Johnson if he could talk to the boys about a business deal.

"Mr. Johnson said yes. Dad took the boys over by the car in full view of their father.

"He said, 'I know that you are the ones that took food from our house, but I am not here to embarrass you in front of your parents. Please promise to never steal from us again. If you need something, just ask.'

"They went back over to Mr. Johnson, and Dad told him, 'I hope you don't mind as a good neighbor we have brought some food from our storeroom. I also want to ask your permission for the boys to come work on our farm once or twice a week for five dollars an hour.'

"Mr. Johnson was very pleased and thanked all of us for our generosity. 'If you ever need anything please don't hesitate to ask,' he said.

"We all learned a valuable lesson that day on how to treat people with respect."

"How do think that would have been handled today?"

"Would you have been able to deal with the real need? Or, would you have freaked out?"

You might say it was food for thought. As Mike drove home, he thought about how he might have handled it. He also thought about the real lesson he had learned and said a prayer that he might have that kind of wisdom.

57

EXERCISE

M ike didn't often preach at church. He preferred
to work one-on-one with people where he could
say what was needed to really help them. One Sunday
he was asked to preach at mass about the truck stop
ministry. He wrote the following article afterward for
the Sunday bulletin.

Do you need Exercise?

Do you feel fatigued and have a lack of
energy? Maybe you need exercise to get your
body's engine working better. When we exercise,
we use muscles that have been relaxed for too
long and have gotten weak. These muscles
respond to the workout, and they become
strengthened. In addition, Nature gives us
additional strength in the form of endorphins.
The result is an overall feeling of well-being.
An exercise program can however, be difficult
to start, but once we start, we begin to feel the
results and become encouraged to continue.
Very often we say that we are too busy to do

something new, but in fact what we really need is something new.

Our faith sometimes needs exercise also to become strengthened. It is a proven fact that when we exercise our faith, we become happier and we find it easier to face each day, because of the strength of faith in our daily lives. We exercise our faith when we spend time with those that we love, when we pray, and when we help others.

My name is Deacon, Michael (Mike) O'Toole, Truck Stop Chaplain. I am asking that you consider an exercise program for your faith. The exercise can be done at several locations in your parish, just call the parish office and ask if you can help with activities in the parish or with the Truck Stop Ministry. Remember, you are in control. You say when and how much you want to help, because we understand your busy life.

I would like to suggest a simple activity that will help you to get started. Help out as a Truck Stop Chaplain assistant. Don't let the title get you frightened. This is a ministry of presence to the truckers and travelers. The ministry is simply being there and present to the people and available to them if they want to talk. These lonely people are very appreciative of the fact that you are there to spend time to talk with them. Sometimes, they want to talk about their family, about their crazy day, or about deeper issues. You don't have to solve anything, or be an expert on religion, just listen and be interested. The following is an example thank-you letter I received:

Dear Michael,

We met at the truck stop a few weeks ago. I was picking up my mom for a visit and you were talking with her and my dad....

Thank you for your spirit, passion and the work you do. The idea of how you minister to those weary men and women has stayed with me. It has enhanced my own faith journey. Please know that your work makes a difference and I see they appreciate that you walk the earth.

When people say, "What would Jesus do?" I believe he would hang out in a truck stop drink strong coffee, and pass the time with those we don't care to notice.

God be with you.
A.........

How many people have you seen, "But, didn't care to notice?"

We have all heard that we need to exercise to keep our hearts strong and our bodies healthy. Please also consider doing some exercise to keep your faith strong and your spiritual body healthy.

God Bless you,
Deacon Mike

58

THE INTERRUPTER

M ike wrote in his journal, *Ken was a man of thirty-eight with a muscular build and a full head of light brown hair. There I go with that hair thing again.*

In looking at Ken, you wouldn't think he had a care in the world. He was always smiling. He was the kind of person that you would automatically say hello to. Apparently he had been at this truck stop often because three waitresses came over to say hello. It didn't seem to be a flirty kind of greeting. Ken's voice was soft, not loud and gregarious, just genuinely friendly.

Ken was in a booth next to the counter, and Mike noticed that a younger man sat across from him. They had finished their meal and paid the waitress.

Mike started his rounds as the younger man was leaving the booth. Ken turned as the Chaplain said, "Hello."

Mike did the usual introductions then Ken said, "Do you have a few minutes? I have something I need to discuss with you."

"Sure do."

"Well, I have had some real problems with my daughter Chelsea, who is only fifteen years old, but has been hanging around with a boy who is eighteen. My being on the road so much isn't helping at all and my wife is about to lose it. I don't know what to do."

Mike started to ask a question to get to the root of the problem, but as he opened his mouth, the other younger man returned to the booth and looked at Mike's nametag and said, "Hi, Chaplain, my name is Aaron. I am Ken's student driver. So you might say that we are sort of joined at the hip for at least the next three weeks."

Aaron's voice was loud as he talked in a kind of machine gun fashion. Mike could tell the man liked to be the center of attention. For the next ten minutes, Mike tried to gently shut the young man down and continue his conversation with Ken but was not successful.

Ken was not happy and finally said, "We have to get back on the road to keep on schedule."

He thanked the chaplain and said, "I'm sorry it didn't work out, but we have to go."

Mike could tell Ken was not happy, so he gave Ken his card and said, "Call me."

Mike gave them a quick blessing and told Ken he would pray for him and Chelsea. Ken thanked him and left with his student.

This was one of those times when someone wanted to talk at a deeper level but someone else kept monopolizing the conversation. Mike felt totally frustrated and at a loss. He wanted so much to talk with Ken about his wife and daughter to see if he could help the man, but the student and the schedule got in the way.

Mike never heard back from Ken and never saw him again. The waitresses told him that Ken had been in on other nights, but Mike had not been there at the same time.

These were the situations when Michael really second guessed himself.

"Did I say the right things? Was there something else I could have done? Maybe I should have asked the student to shut up or sent him away."

These were regrets in his head, but the reality was that if Ken had really wanted to talk he would have made time and sent the student to the truck for a couple of minutes. It would have probably been out of bounds and too pushy for Mike to suggest those same things. He had planted a seed in Ken that someone was interested in listening. Perhaps he would seek out another chaplain for help.

Mike told Mandy that evening, "I sometimes get a feeling of frustration after I leave the truck stop that I did not get to everyone. So, I start second guessing what I have done and said."

"You are going to have to get over it and just accept what happens each week as the work of the Holy Spirit. I think you are talking with those you are supposed to be talking with and saying what you are supposed to say," Mandy expressed with empathy.

"You should not be frustrated if you only get a chance to talk to a few people each night. After all, some of those conversations have been very rewarding and helpful."

"I know that I have brought some peace and hope to them by listening and being interested in their struggles, problems, and happiness. I guess I always think I could have done more."

Mike told his good friend Ron the story and said, "Be honest with yourself. How many times have you started a conversation with someone and immediately started thinking of what you wanted to say next, instead of listening to what they were really saying? Have you ever been caught?"

"Yes, I have. Someone was talking to me and telling me some details, then they asked me a question about it. I was embarrassed, because I had no idea what they were saying.

"Another one was someone was talking to me, and someone else said hello to both of us. When the other person left, the first person turned back to me, and said, 'I lost my train of thought. Where were we?' I was at a loss, because I wasn't paying attention in the first place. Oops!"

Mike added, "The other day, my wife said, 'I don't think you heard a word I've said.'"

"We're human, and we are constantly thinking. So it is a real challenge to actively listen to others and ask them questions about what they are saying to get to the heart of the matter," Ron told Mike.

Mike lamented, "For many of us, the temptation is to just give the *solution pill*, or the quick answer to their problem that will get them off of the subject, instead of asking questions and helping them to realize their own solution. I admit there are those situations where you have to use these tactics. But, it is amazing, when you practice active listening and get involved in a person's pain or happiness, how that can energize you as you help them find answers and themselves."

59

SHE STARTED TO CRY

Mike walked up to a booth of an older man and woman, and said, "Hi, I'm the Chaplain here..."

Before he could get the rest of his intro out, the woman immediately started to cry.

He asked, "What's wrong?"

She said, "That is amazing!"

"What do you mean?"

"We have been working on a serious problem, and we just said a prayer that the Lord would send us help and guidance, then...there you were."

That put a smile on Mike's face at the thought. But, their words stopped him speechless for a moment, to think that he might be a message from the Lord to these people in need.

He finally said, "Wow! That's a pretty tall order! How can I help?"

"You already have. Please sit with us."

She moved over to let him sit down, and then the couple took turns explaining.

"My name is Alice and my husband is Randy. We had just been discussing what to do with our home. You see, our children are all grown and have moved away. The two of us are on the road, and we were discussing whether we should sell the house where we raised our kids."

"How long have you been traveling together?"

"Two years."

"Do you get along well, trapped in that metal box out there?

"Yes, although there have been a couple of disagreements, but nothing major."

"Are you both healthy?"

"Yes. No major illnesses."

"Well, it sounds like it should work. Where would you call home?"

"We'd get a small apartment near one of our kids."

"It sounds like you have it all worked out. Do you both drive?"

"No, not yet. Only Randy drives. I am just along for company, but I am thinking I should learn."

"We could make a lot more money. And that was the other thing we were praying about," Randy said.

"So, what do you think?" asked Alice.

Randy looked at his wife and said cautiously, "It sounds like we have no real reason to keep the house."

Then he said, "We should sell it and get a small place near Jim and Ellyn and our grandkids."

"I agree, and I will start learning to drive. I am really exited that we had your help, Chaplain," she said.

"Well, I didn't really do anything, except listen."

"Thank you for being here and for spending your time with us. God Bless you. We will pray for you that you keep doing this ministry. We drivers really need you."

Mike said a prayer with them, as they piled their hands in a loving embrace in the middle of the table. They all started to laugh at the same time, partly for the joy they felt and partly for the fact that our pile of hands reminded them of a kid's game.

He said, "It reminds me of the game we played when I wore a younger man's clothes."

They all laughed and talked about it for a while then they said good-bye.

When Mike stood up, they got up with him and each gave him a warm and loving hug.

Mike later told his wife, "It's amazing to me how close you can get to a couple in only an hour of sharing their hopes and dreams and human emotions. All three of us were on an emotional high and went floating out of the truck stop. Each of us was on a separate path, but a common path in the name of the Lord.

"I didn't need to use pushiness or a formula or an agenda, just a mutual respect and sharing of ideas feelings and emotions. We had formed a four-way relationship with each other and the Lord at the center of our thoughts, our hearts, and our spirits, and we all gained from the relationship we formed with each other tonight."

Amen?

Amen!

EPILOGUE

The stories you have just experienced are based on the real Truck Stop Ministry of the author, Rich Seveska. The fictional character Michael O'Toole was invented to facilitate story telling and the stories were developed around Mike as the chaplain. Some of the stories are verbatim accounts of the actual events, like, *The Hills* and *The Orchard*, while others were based on a theme.

The author currently lives with his wife JoAnn, in Orange Beach, Alabama and has retired from the ministry.

He hopes you have enjoyed the stories and have gained a closer relationship with God, yourself, and all those around you.